eForth Overview

Chen-Hanson Ting

This Book is Copyright © ExMark, 03 October 2018

The current Forth Bookshelf can be found at
https://www.amazon.co.uk/Juergen-Pintaske/e/B00N8HVEZM

All 20 available as eBook. The P after the number notes available as print book as well

1_   **Charles Moore** - Forth - The Early Years: Background information about the beginnings of this Computer Language

2P   **Charles Moore** - Programming A Problem Oriented Language: Forth - how the internals work

3_   **Leo Brodie** - Starting Forth -The Classic

4P   **Leo Wong – Juergen Pintaske – Stephen Pelc** FORTH LITE TUTORIAL: Code tested with free MPE VFX Forth, SwiftForth and Gforth or else

5P   **Juergen Pintaske – A START WITH FORTH** - Bits to Bites Collection – 12 Words to start, then 35 Words, Javascript Forth on the Web, more

6P   **Stephen Pelc** - Programming Forth: Version July 2016

7P   **Brad Rodriguez** - Moving Forth / TTL CPU / B.Y.O. Assembler

8_   **Tim Hentlass** - Real Time Forth

9P   **Chen-Hanson Ting** - Footsteps In An Empty Valley issue 3

10   **Chen-Hanson Ting** - Zen and the Forth Language: EFORTH for the MSP430G2552 from Texas Instruments

11_   **Chen-Hanson Ting** - eForth and Zen - 3rd Edition 2017: with 32-bit 86eForth v5.2 for Visual Studio 2015

12P   **Chen-Hanson Ting** - eForth Overview

13_   **Chen-Hanson Ting** - FIG-Forth Manual Document /Test in 1802 IP

14_   **Chen-Hanson Ting** - EP32 RISC Processor IP: Description and Implementation into FPGA – ASIC tested by NASA

15_   **Chen-Hanson Ting** – Irriducible Complexity

16_   **Chen-Hanson Ting** - Arduino controlled by eForth

17_   **Burkhard Kainka** - Learning Programming with MyCo: Learning Programming easily - independent of a PC (Forth code to follow soon)

18_   **Burkhard Kainka** - BBC Micro:bit: Tests Tricks Secrets Code, Additional MicroBit information when running the Mecrisp Package

19_   **Burkhard Kainka / Thomas Baum** – Web Programming TINY13 – Lars tried Forth

20P   **Georg Heinrichs** - The ATTINY 2313 Project – Why Forth?

Contents

Additional Material for download and print can be found at
https://wiki.forth-ev.de/doku.php/en:projects:430eforth:start

There you can find the complete code from this book on one page.
The size is about 60 x 75 cm – but many print shops will do it.
The same as the picture shown on page 1.
Alternatively, normal printout, combine pages using sticky tape.

File: eForth_Overview_2016_09_07_v4a_2016_10_19

1.0 eForth Overview

Before diving directly into eForth, I would like to discuss the general principles of Forth language. The language consists of a collection of words, which reside in the memory of a computer and can be executed by entering their names on the computer keyboard. A list of words can be compiled, given a new name and made a new word. In fact, most words in Forth are defined as lists of existing words. A small set of primitive words are defined in machine code of the native CPU. All other words are built from these primitive words and eventually refer to them when executed.

Words are similar to procedures and subroutines in other languages. The difference is that Forth words are executable interactively when referenced by name, and they can be compiled into lists which can be referenced as new words. Programming in Forth is to define new and more powerful words as lists of existing words. This process continues until the final word becomes the solution to an application. Here I will state 'The Forth Law of Computing" without a proof:

All computable functions can be constructed by defining new words as lists of words which include a small number of primitive words.

This eForth model consists of about 200 words, of which only 31 are primitive words. Although it is very difficult to prove the above law, I will demonstrate it to you that from this small set of primitive words a complete operating system with many tools, that is the eForth model itself, can be built. If an operating system can be built this way, it is not difficult to understand that any application can be so developed.

Forth is very similar to machine code. In a computer, the CPU has a finite set of machine instructions, and all computable functions are implemented as lists of these machine instructions. High level languages generally replace machine instruction lists by statements, functions, subroutines, and procedures, which can be used to construct procedures and subroutines at higher levels until the last procedure which is the application. This also helps demonstrating the validity of the above law.

The primitive words must be constructed using native machine code of the host computer. They are also called low level words or code words. All other words are constructed as lists of existing words. They are called high level words or colon words because ":" (colon) is a Forth word which defines or constructs new words to replace lists of existing words.

Forth as a computing system has two principal components: a user interface as the Forth language processor which interprets the commands entered from keyboard or equivalent devices; and a machine interface which interprets lists or words recursively until it can issue machine instructions in the primitive words to the host computer for execution. The user interface processes commands in text form. It is often referred to as the text interpreter and the outer interpreter.

The machine interface executes words by processing recursively the word lists compiled in colon words to reach the primitive words which are handed to the host computer for execution. It is often called the inner interpreter and the address interpreter, because the word lists are often stored in the dictionary as address lists.

1.1 Virtual Forth Computer

Forth is a computer model which can be implemented on any real CPU with reasonable resources. This model is often called a virtual Forth computer. The minimal components of a virtual Forth computer are:
1. A dictionary in memory to hold all the execution procedures.
2. A return stack to hold return addresses of procedures yet to be executed.
3. A data stack to hold parameters passing between procedures.
4. A user area in RAM memory to hold all the system variables.
5. A CPU to move date among stacks and memory, and to do ALU operations to parameters stored on the data stack.

The eForth model is a detailed specification of a virtual Forth computer which can be implemented on many different CPU's and forces them to behave identically in executing an identical Forth instruction set. It was first implemneted on a PC using Intel 8086 CPU as a guiding model for other implementations. Here we will try to describe precisely the behavior of the virtual Forth computer. To describe precisely how this computer functions, we will use the 8086 machine code to clarify the specification.

The following registers are required for a virtual Forth computer:

Forth Register	8086 Register	Function
IP	SI	Interpreter Pointer
SP	SP	Data Stack Pointer
RP	RP	Return Stack Pointer
WP	AX	Word or Work Pointer
UP	(in memory)	User Area Pointer

In the dictionary, each procedure (or word in Forth terminology) occupies an area called code field, which contains executable machine code and data required by the code. There are two types of words used in eForth: code word whose code field contains only machine instructions, and colon word whose code field contains a call to the list processing subroutine and a list of word addresses. A word address is the code field address of the word in the dictionary. 4 bytes are allocated for the call to list processor. Word addresses are 2 bytes in length and are pointers to code fields of words in the dictionary. The length of a code field varies depending upon the complexity of the word.

In the code field of a code word there is a list of machine instructions of the native CPU. The machine instructions are terminated by a group of instructions, generally specified as a macro instruction named $NEXT. The function of $NEXT is to fetch the next word pointed to by the Interpreter Pointer IP, increment IP to point to the next word in the word list, and jump to the address just fetched.

Since a word address points to a code field containing executable machine instructions, executing a word means jumping directly to the code field pointed to by the word address. $NEXT thus allows the virtual Forth computer to execute a list of words with very little CPU overhead. In the 8086 implementation, $NEXT is a macro assembling the following two machine instructions as shown below.

In a colon word, the first four bytes in the code field must be a subroutine call instruction to process the address list following this call instruction. This address list processing subroutine is named doLIST. doLIST pushes the contents in IP onto the return stack, copies the address of the first entry in its address list into IP and then calls $NEXT. $NEXT will then start executing this list of addresses in sequence.

The last entry in the address list of a colon word must be EXIT. EXIT is a code word which undoes what doLIST accomplished. EXIT pops the top item on the return stack into the IP register. Consequently, IP points to the address following the colon word just executed. EXIT then invokes $NEXT which continues the processing of the word list, briefly interrupted by the last colon word in this word list.

```
$NEXT   MACRO (IP, WP) // SI, AX
        LODSW       \ load next word into WP (AX)    Load SI into AX
        JMP AX      \ jump directly to the word thru WP    increment SI
        ENDM  \ IP (SI) now points to the next word


doLIST ( a -- )     \ Run address list in a colon word
        XCHG  BP,SP  \ exchange pointers
        PUSH  SI     \ push return stack
        XCHG  BP,SP  \ restore the pointers
        POP   SI     \ new list address
        $NEXT


CODE    EXIT         \ Terminate a colon definition.
        XCHG  BP,SP  \ exchange pointers
        POP   SI     \ pop return stack
        XCHG  BP,SP  \ restore the pointers
        $NEXT
```

It is interesting to note that in this eForth implementation, $NEXT is a macro, doLIST is a subroutine, and EXIT is actually a Forth code word. $NEXT, doLIST and EXIT are collectively call the 'inner interpreters' and 'address interpreters' of Forth. They are the corner stones of a virtual Forth computer as they control the execution flow of Forth words in the system.

Based on the above mechanism to execute code words and colon words, a Forth computer can be constructed using a small set of machine dependent code words and a much larger set of colon words. Tools are provided so that the user can extend the system by adding new words in truly modular fashion to solve any practical problems. There are 190 high level words in eForth, built on the 31 low level primitive words.

The high-level word set is required to build the outer interpreter and the associated utility words. As the outer interpreter itself represents a fairly substantial application, the word set necessary to build the outer interpreter forms a very solid foundation to build most other applications. However, for any real-world application one would not expect that this eForth word set is sufficient.

The beauty of Forth is that in programming an application, the user designs and implements a new word set best tailored to his application. Forth is an open system, assuming that no operating system can be complete and all-encompassing. The user has the best understanding of his own needs, and he knows the best way to accomplish his goal.

1.2 Memory Map

The most important contribution by von Neumann to the computer design was the recognition that a single, uniform memory device can be used to store program and data, contrasting to the then prevailing architectures in which program and data were stored separately and most often using very different storage media. It greatly simplified the design of computers and had become the dominant computer architecture for all the important computer families ever since.

Memory space is a concept of paramount importance in computer hardware and assembly programming, but often hidden and ignored in most conventional high-level languages. High level languages and operating systems hide the addressable memory space from the user in order to protect the operating system, because there are very sensitive areas in the memory space and unintentional alterations to the information stored in these areas would cause the system to malfunction or even to crash.

The point of view from the operating system and from the computer priesthood, these sensitive areas must be protected at all cost, and they are the reserved territory of the systems programmers. Ordinary applications programmers are allocated only enough space to run their programs safely, for their own good.

Forth opens the entire memory space to the user. The user can freely store data and code into memory and retrieve them from the memory. Coming with the freedom is the responsibility of handling the memory correctly.

Memory used in eForth is separated into the following areas:

Cold boot	100H-	17FH	Cold start and variable initial values
Code dictionary	180H-	1344H	Code dictionary growing upward
Free space	1346H-	33E4H	Shared by code/name dictionaries
Name/word	33E6H-	3BFFH	Name dictionary growing downward
Data stack	3C00H-	3E7FH	Growing downward
TIB	3E80H-		Growing upward
Return stack		-3F7FH	Growing downward
User variables	3F80H-	3FFFH	

These areas are allocated by assembly constants and can be changed conveniently to suit the target environment. The following assembly code segment prescribes the memory allocation in a typical eForth system. The memory map is also illustrated in a schematic drawing for easier visulization.

```
;; Memory allocation
;; 0//code>--//--<name//up>--<sp//tib>--rp//em
EM      EQU     04000H          ;top of memory
COLDD   EQU     00100H          ;cold start vector
US      EQU     64*CELLL        ;user area size in cells
RTS     EQU     64*CELLL        ;return stack/TIB size
RPP     EQU     EM-8*CELLL      ;start of return stack (RP0)
TIBB    EQU     RPP-RTS         ;terminal input buffer (TIB)
SPP     EQU     TIBB-8*CELLL    ;start of data stack (SP0)
UPP     EQU     EM-256*CELLL    ;start of user area (UP0)
NAMEE   EQU     UPP-8*CELLL     ;name dictionary
CODEE   EQU     COLDD+US        ;code dictionary
```

2.0 eForth Kernel — The kernel words

One of the most important features of eForth is the small machine dependent kernel, which allows its to be ported to other CPUs very conveniently. The selection of words in this kernel is based on the criteria that they are very difficult if not impossible to synthesize from other primitive words. From this set of kernel words, all other Forth words have to be built.

The 31 kernel words can be classified as following:

2.1 16

System interface:	BYE	?rx	tx!	!io
Inner interpreters:	doLIT	doLIST	next	?branch
	Branch	EXECUTE	EXIT	
Memory access:	!	@	C!	C@
Return stack:	RP@	RP!	R>	R>	R@
Data stack:	SP@	SP!	DROP	DUP
	SWAP	OVER		
Logic:	0<	AND	OR	XOR
Arithmetic:	UM+			

2.2
18 2.3 21
4 23

The virtual Forth computer is based on a two-stack architecture. The return stack is used to allow a high-level word to be executed in the address list of another high-level word. It is very similar to the return stack used for nested subroutine calls in a conventional computer. Before executing a high-level word in an address list, the next address of the list is pushed on the return stack so that the IP register can be used to scan the address list in the called word.

When the called word is executed to completion, the stored address on the returned stack is popped back into IP register and execution of the calling word list can be continued.

The data stack is used to pass parameters from one word to another. Conventional computers use the return stack to do the parameter passing, and it takes a very complicated compiler to figure out which are return addresses, and which are parameters. Forth segregated these two types of information on two separate stacks and thus greatly simplies the execution and compilation of words.

Passing parameter on the data stack also reduces the syntactical complexity of Forth language to the minimum and allows words to be strung together into lists with minimum overhead in compilation and interpretation.

The kernal words move and process data and address among the stacks and the memory. They emcompass the minimal functionality necessary to make a computer to behave like a Forth computer. A complete understanding of these kernel words is vital, to the understanding of a virtual Forth computer. However, it is not difficult to understand the kernel words, because there are only 31 of them.

It is my intention to use this eForth model to illustrate the validity of 'the Forth Law of Computing', which stated that all computable functions can be constructed by lists of these kernel words and the high-level words built from these kernel words. The eForth model includes a text interpreter which allows the user to type lists of word names and execute them in sequence, a compiler which allows the user to name lists of words and compile new words, and utilities like memory dump, stack dump, and a colon word decompiler.

Thus, the eForth system forms a fairly complete software development environment for the user to develop applications. If such a system can be built from this small set of kernel words, it should be obvious that most practical applications can also be built from it.

2.1 System Interface

BYE returns control from eForth back to the operating system. !io initializes the serial I/O device in the system so that it can interact with the user through a terminal. These two words are not needed once the eForth system is up and running, but they are essential to bring the system up in DOS. ?rx is used to implement ?KEY and KEY, and tx! is used to implement EMIT. eForth communicates with the user through these words which supports terminal interactions and file download/upload. Here these words are defined using the DOS service calls. For embedded controllers, these three words must be defined for the specific I/O devices.

?RX is a unique design invented by Bill Muench to support serial input . ?RX provides the functions required of both KEY and KEY? which accept input from a terminal. ?RX inspects the terminal device and returns a character and a true flag if the character has been received and is waiting to be retrieved. If no character was received, ?RX simply returns a false flag. With ?RX, both KEY and KEY? can be defined as high level colon definitions.

TX! sends a character on the data stack to the terminal device. Both ?RX and TX! are coded here as DOS calls. In embedded applications, they will have to be coded in machine specific code to handle the specific serial I/O device.

!IO initializes the serial I/O device, which is not necessary here because it is taking care of by the DOS. In embedded systems, the I/O device must be initialized by !IO.

```
CODE  BYE      ( -- , exit Forth )
      INT      020H              \ return to DOS

CODE  ?RX      ( -- c T | F )  \ Return input character and true,
                               \ or a false if no input.
      $CODE    3,'?RX',QRX
      XOR      BX,BX            \ BX=0 setup for false flag
      MOV      DL,0FFH          \ input command
      MOV      AH,6             \ MS-DOS Direct Console I/O
      INT      021H
      JZ       QRX3             \ ?key ready
      OR       AL,AL            \ AL=0 if extended char
      JNZ      QRX1             \ ?extended character code
      INT      021H
      MOV      BH,AL            \ extended code in msb
      JMP      QRX2
QRX1: MOV      BL,AL
QRX2: PUSH     BX               \ save character
      MOV      BX,-1            \ true flag
QRX3: PUSH     BX
      $NEXT

CODE  TX!      ( c -- )   \ Send character c to output device.
      POP      DX               \ char in DL
      CMP      DL,0FFH          \ 0FFH is interpreted as input
      JNZ      TX1              \ do NOT allow input
      MOV      DL,32            \ change to blank
TX1:  MOV      AH,6             \ MS-DOS Direct Console I/O
      INT      021H             \ display character
      $NEXT

CODE  !IO      ( -- )     \ Initialize the serial I/O devices.
      $NEXT
```

2.2 Inner Interpreter

In the word list of a colon definition, it is generally assumed that words are execution addresses, which can be executed sequentially by the address interpreter $NEXT. However, occasionally we do need to compile other types of data in-line with the words.

Special mechanisms must be used to tell the address interpreter to treat these data differently. All data entries must be preceded by special words which can handle the data properly. A special word and its associated data form a data structure. Data structures are extensions of words and can be thought of as building blocks to form lists in colon definitions.

$NEXT must be assembled at the end of a code word. It fetches the next address in the address list pointed to by IP and jumps to that address. It allows an address list to be scanned and thus executed. doLIST starts the execution of an address list by saving IP on the return stack and stores the starting address of an address list into IP, and then $NEXT starts executing this address list.

EXIT must be compiled as the last entry in an address list. It terminates the execution of the current address list and returns execution to the address saved on the return stack.

EXECUTE takes the execution address from the data stack and executes that word. This powerful word allows the user to execute any word which is not part of an address list.

doLIT pushes the next word onto the data stack as an integer literal instead of as an address to be executed by $NEXT. It allows numbers to be compiled as in-line literals, supplying data to the data stack at run time. doLIT is not used by itself, but rather compiled by LITERAL which inserts doLIT and its asociated integer into the address list under construction. Anytime you see a number in a colon definition, LITERAL is invoked to compile an integer literal with doLIT.

Integer literals are by far the most numerous data structures in colon definitions other than regular words. Address literals are used to build control structures. String literals are used to embed text strings in colon definitions.

```
$NEXT   MACRO
        LODSW           \ load next word into WP (AX)
        JMP     AX      \ jump directly to the word thru WP
        ENDM            \ IP (SI) now points to the next word

doLIST  ( a -- )        \ Run address list in a colon word.
        XCHG    BP,SP   \ exchange pointers
        PUSH    SI      \ push return stack
        XCHG    BP,SP   \ restore the pointers
        POP     SI      \ new list address
        $NEXT

CODE    EXIT            \ Terminate a colon definition.
        XCHG    BP,SP   \ exchange pointers
        POP     SI      \ pop return stack
        XCHG    BP,SP   \ restore the pointers
        $NEXT

CODE    EXECUTE    ( ca -- )    \ Execute the word at ca.
        POP     BX
        JMP     BX      \ jump to the code address

CODE    doLIT   ( -- w )    \ Push inline literal on data stack.
```

```
LODSW              \ get the literal compiled in-line
PUSH  AX           \ push literal on the stack
$NEXT              \ execute next word after literal
```

2.3 Loops and Branches

eForth uses three different types of address literals. 'next', '?branch' and 'branch' are followed not by word addresses but by pointers to locations in a list to be executed next. These address literals are the building blocks upon which loops, and branching structures are constructed. An address literal is followed by a branch pointer which causes execution to be transferred to that location. The branch location most often points to a different location in the address list of the same colon word.

```
CODE    next ( -- )        \ Decrement index and exit loop
                           \ if index is less than 0.
        SUB    WORD PTR [BP],1    \ decrement the index
        JC     NEXT1             \ ?decrement below 0
        MOV    SI,0[SI]          \ no, continue loop
        $NEXT
NEXT1:  ADD    BP,2    \ yes, pop the index
        ADD    SI,2    \ exit loop
        $NEXT


CODE    ?branch ( f -- )    \ Branch if flag is zero.
        POP    BX               \ pop flag
        OR     BX,BX            \ ?flag=0
        JZ     BRAN1            \ yes, so branch
        ADD    SI,2             \ point IP to next cell
        $NEXT
BRAN1:  MOV    SI,0[SI]         \ IP:=(IP), jump to new address
        $NEXT

CODE    branch ( -- )       \ Branch to an inline address.
        MOV    SI,0[SI]          \ jump to new address unconditionally
        $NEXT
```

Address literals are used to construct control structures in colon definitions. 'next' is compiled by NEXT. '?branch' is compiled by IF, WHILE and UNTIL. 'branch' is compiled by AFT, ELSE, REPEAT and AGAIN. In the colon words to be discussed in the later sections, you will not see these kernel words but words which construct loops and branches. For example:

IF	(compiles ?branch and address after THEN)	\<true clause\> THEN
IF	(compiles ?branch and address after ELSE)	\<true clause\>
ELSE	(compiles branch and address after THEN)	\<false clause\> THEN
BEGIN	(marks current address)	\<loop clause\>
AGAIN	(compiles branch and address after BEGIN)	
BEGIN	(mark current address)	\<loop clause\>
UNTIL	(compiles ?branch and address after BEGIN)	
BEGIN	(mark current address)	\<loop clause\>
WHILE	(compiles ?branch and address after REPEAT)	\<true clause\>
REPEAT	(compile branch and address after BEGIN)	
FOR	(set up loop, mark current address)	\<loop clause\>
NEXT	(compile next and address after FOR)	
FOR	(set up loop, mark current address)	\<loopclause\>
AFT	(change marked address to current address, compile branch and address after THEN)	\<skip clause\>
THEN	\<loop clause\> NEXT (compile next and address after AFT)	

NEXT   next

IF, WHILE, UNTIL   ? branch

AFT, ELSE, REPEAT, AGAIN   branch

2.4 Memory Access

Four memory accessing words are included in the eForth kernel:

> `!` `(store)`, `@` `(fetch)`, `C!` `(C-store)` and `C@` `(C-fetch)`.

`!` and `@` access memory in cells, whose size depends on the CPU underneath. eForth assumes that the CPU can access memory in bytes and that all addresses are in the units of bytes. `C!` and `C@` allow the user access memory in bytes.

The two most important resources in a computer are the CPU and the memory. There is not much one can do with the CPU, except to use its instruction set to write programs. However, the real usefulness and intelligence lies with the memory, which holds both the program and the data. In conventional languages, you humbly request memory to store your data, and the compiler reluctantly allocate it to you. If you exceed your memory allocation, your program will be ruthlessly terminated.

In Forth, you have all the memory and you are allowed to do anything with the memory. `!`, `@`, `C!` and `C@` do not place restriction on their use. You can use them to write self-modifying code if you like. However, you must know exactly what you are doing.

It is not a very good idea to change the contents of the dictionary, except in the parameter fields of variables and arrays you defined specifically for data storage. The space occupied by the stacks should be respected, too. The user variable area holds vital information for the system to run correctly. The space bewteen the code dictionary and the name dictionary are not used, and you are free to use it to store temporary data.

Be reminded, however, that as you define new words, the dictionaries are extended and may over-write data you placed there.

The moral is: Use @ and C@ freely, but be careful with ! and C!.

```
CODE    !  ( w a -- )    \ Pop the data stack to memory.
        POP    BX         \ get address from tos
        POP    0[BX]      \ store data to that adddress
        $NEXT


CODE    @  ( a -- w )    \ Push memory location to data stack.
        POP    BX         \ get address
        PUSH   0[BX]      \ fetch data
        $NEXT


CODE    C!  ( c b -- )   \ Pop data stack to byte memory.
        POP    BX         \ get address
        POP    AX         \ get data in a cell
        MOV    0[BX],AL   \ store one byte
        $NEXT


CODE    C@  ( b -- c )  \ Push byte memory content on data stack.
        POP    BX         \ get address
        XOR    AX,AX      \ AX=0 zero the hi byte
        MOV    AL,0[BX]   \ get low byte
        PUSH   AX         \ push on stack
        $NEXT
```

2.5 Return Stack

RP! pushes the address on the top of the data stack to the return stack and thus initializes the return stack. RP! is only used to initialize the system and are seldom used in applications. RP@ pushes the contents of the return stack pointer RP on the data stack. It is also used very rarely in applications.

>R pops a number off the data stack and pushes it on the return stack.. R> does the opposite. R@ copies the top item on the return stack and pushes it on the data stack.

The eForth system uses the return stack for two specific purposes: to save addresses while recusing through an address list, and to store the loop index during a FOR-NEXT loop. As the addresses piled up on the return stack changes dynamically as words are executed, there is very little useful information the user can get from the return stack at the run time.

In setting up a loop, FOR compiles >R, which pushes the loop index from the data stack to the return stack. Inside the FOR-NEXT loop, the running index can be recalled by R@. NEXT compiles 'next' with an address after FOR. when 'next' is executed, it decrements the loop index on the top of the return stack. If the index becomes negative, the loop is terminated; otherwise, 'next' jumps back to the word after FOR.

Return stack is used by the virtual Forth computer to save return addresses to be processes later. It is also a convenient place to store data temporarily. The return stack can thus be considered as a extension of the data stack. However, one must be very careful in using the return stack for temporary storage. The data pushed on the return stack must be popped off before EXIT is executed. Otherwise, EXIT will get the wrong address to return to, and the system generally will crash.

```
CODE    RP@   ( -- a )   \ Push current RP to data stack.
        PUSH  BP              \ copy address to return stack
        $NEXT                \ pointer register BP

CODE    RP!   ( a -- )   \ Set the return stack pointer.
        POP   BP             \ copy (BP) to tos
        $NEXT

CODE    R>    ( -- w )   \ Pop return stack to data stack.
        PUSH  0[BP]         \ copy w to data stack
        ADD   BP,2          \ adjust RP for popping
        $NEXT

CODE    R@    ( -- w )   \ Copy top of return stack to data stack.
        PUSH  0[BP]         \ copy w to data stack
        $NEXT

CODE    >R    ( w -- )   \ Push data stack to return stack.
        SUB   BP,2          \ adjust RP for pushing
        POP   0[BP]         \ push w to return stack
        $NEXT
```

2.6 Data Stack

The data stack is the centralized location where all numerical data are processed, and where parameters are passed from one word to another. The stack items have to be arranged properly so that they can be retrieved properly in the Last-In-First-Out (LIFO) manner. When stack items are out of order, they can be rearranged by the stack words DUP, SWAP, OVER and DROP. There are other stack words useful in manipulating stack items, but these four are considered to be the minimum set.

Data stack is initialized by SP!. The depth of data stack can be examined by SP@. These words, as RP@ and RP! are only used by the system and very rarely used in applications. These words are necessary in the Forth kernel because you cannot operate a stack-based computer without these instructions.

```
CODE    DROP      ( w -- )   \ Discard top stack item.    As stack
        ADD    SP,2             \ adjust SP to pop      grows down
        $NEXT


CODE    DUP    ( w -- w w )  \ Duplicate the top stack item.
        MOV    BX,SP            \ use BX to index the stack
        PUSH   0[BX]                    Put SP in BX
        $NEXT                           Push BX


CODE    SWAP ( w1 w2 -- w2 w1 )   \ Exchange top two stack items.
        POP    BX              \ get w2
        POP    AX              \ get w1
        PUSH   BX              \ push w2
        PUSH   AX               \ push w1
        $NEXT
```

```
CODE     OVER ( w1 w2 -- w1 w2 w1 ) \ Copy second stack item
                                     \ to top.
         MOV    BX,SP        \ use BX to index the stack
         PUSH   2[BX]        \ get w1 and push on stack
         $NEXT

CODE     SP@ ( -- a )    \ Push the current data stack pointer.
         MOV    BX,SP        \ use BX to index the stack
         PUSH   BX           \ push SP back
         $NEXT

CODE     SP! ( a -- ) \ Set the data stack pointer.
         POP    SP           \ safety
         $NEXT
```

·depth

?

Data Stack

SP →   grows down

2.7 Logical Words

The only primitive word which cares about logic is '?branch'. It tests the top item on the stack. If it is zero, ?branch will branch to the following address. If it is not zero, ?branch will ignore the address and execute the word after the branch address. Thus, we distinguish two classes of numbers, zero for 'false' and non-zero for 'true'.

Numbers used this way are called logic flags which can be either true or false. The only primitive word which generates flags is '0<', which examines the top item on the data stack for its negativeness. If it is negative, '0<' will return a -1 for true. If it is 0 or positive, '0<' will return a 0 for false.

The three logic words AND, OR and XOR are bitwise logic operators over the width of a cell. They can be used to operate on real flags (0 and -1) for logic purposes. The user must be aware of the distinct behaviors between the real flags and the generalized flags.

```
CODE    0<  ( n -- f )    \ Return true if n is negative.
        POP    AX
        CWD                      \ sign extend AX into DX
        PUSH   DX                \ push 0 or -1
        $NEXT

CODE    AND  ( w w -- w )  \ Bitwise AND.
        POP    BX
        POP    AX
        AND    BX,AX
        PUSH   BX
        $NEXT
```

```
CODE    OR  ( w w -- w )   \ Bitwise inclusive OR.
        POP    BX
        POP    AX
        OR     BX,AX
        PUSH   BX
        $NEXT

CODE    XOR ( w w -- w )   \ Bitwise exclusive OR.
        POP    BX
        POP    AX
        XOR    BX,AX
        PUSH   BX
        $NEXT
```

2.8 Primitive Arithmetic

The only primitive arithmetic word in the eForth kernel is **UM+**. All other arithmetic words, like +, -, * and / are derived from UM+ as colon definitions. This design emphasizes portability over performance, because it greatly reduces the efforts in moving eForth into CPU's which do not have native multiply and divide instructions. Once eForth is implemented on a new CPU, the more complicated arithmetic words are the first ones to be optimized to enhance the performance.

UM+ adds two unsigned number on the top of the data stack and returns to the data stack the sum of these two numbers and the carry as one number on top of the sum. To handle the carry this way is very inefficient, because most CPU's have carry as a bit in the status register, and the carry can be accessed by many machine instructions. It is thus more convenient to use carry in machine code programming. eForth provides the user a handle on the carry in high level, making it easier for the user to deal with it directly.

```
CODE    UM+    ( w w -- w cy )    \ Add two numbers,
                                  \ return the sum and carry flag.
        XOR    CX,CX              \ CX=0 initial carry flag
        POP    BX
        POP    AX
        ADD    AX,BX
        RCL    CX,1               \ get carry
        PUSH   AX                 \ push sum
        PUSH   CX                 \ push carry
        $NEXT
```

3.0 High Level Forth Words

Following are the eForth words defined as high level colon definitions. They are built from the primitive eForth words and other high level eForth words, including data structures and control structures.

Since eForth source is coded in Microsoft MASM assembler, the word lists in the colon definitions are constructed as data in MASM, using the DW directive. This form of representation, though very effective, is very difficult to read. The original model of eForth as provided by Bill Muench was in the form of a Forth source listing. This listing is much simpler and easy to read, assuming that the reader has some knowledge of the Forth syntax.

This listing is also a very good source to learn a good coding style of Forth. I therefore think it is better to present the high level Forth colon definitions in this form. As the 8086 eForth implementation deviates slightly from the original Forth model, I tried to translate the 8086 implementation faithfully back to the Forth style for our discussion here.

The sequence of words is exactly the same as that in the MASM assembly source listing. The reader is encouraged to read the MASM source listing along with the text in this book. Reading two descriptions of the same subject often enable better comprehension and understanding.

3.1 Variables and User Variables

The term user variable was codified in earlier Forth systems on the mini-computers in which multitasking was an integral part of the Forth operating system. In a multitasking system, many user share CPU and other resources in the computing system. Each user has a private memory area to store essential information about its own task so that the system can leave a task temporarily to serve other users and return to this task continuing the unfinished work. In a single user environment, the user variables have the same functionality as system variables.

In eForth, all variables used by the system are merged together and are implemented uniformly as user variables. A special memory area in the high memory is allocated for all these variables, and they are all initialized by copying a table of initial values stored in the cold boot area. A significant benefit of this scheme is that it allows the eForth system to operate in ROM memory naturally. It is very convenient for embedded system applications which preclude mass storage and file downloading.

In an application, the user can choose to implement variables in the forms of user variables or regular variables when running in RAM memory. To run things in ROM, variables must be defined as user variables. Although eForth in the original model allows only a small number of user variable to be defined in an application, the user area can be enlarged at will by changing a few assembly constants and equates.

In eForth only one vocabulary is used. The name of this vocabulary is FORTH. When FORTH is executed, the address of the pointer to the top of the dictionary is written into the first cell in the CONTEXT array. When the text interpreter searches the dictionary for a words, it picks up the pointer in CONTEXT and follow the thread through the name dictionary.

If the name dictionary is exhausted, the text interpreter will pick up the next cell in the CONTEXT array and do the search. The first cell in CONTEXT array containing a 0 stops the searching. There are 8 cells in the CONTEXT array. Since the last cell must be zero, eForth allows up to 8 context vocabularies to be searched.

There are two empty cells in the code field of FORTH. The first cell stores the pointer to the last name field in the name dictionary. The second field must be a 0, which serves to terminate a vocabulary link when many vocabularies are created.

Vocabularies are useful in reducing the number of words the text interpreter must search to locate a word and allowing related words to be grouped together as logic modules. Although the eForth itself only uses one vocabulary, the mechanism is provided to define multiple vocabularies in large applications.

The CONTEXT arrays is designed as a vocabulary stack to implement the ONLY- ALSO concept of vocabulary search order first proposed by Bill Ragsdale in the Forth 83 Standard.

CURRENT points to a vocabulary thread to which new definitions are to be added.

```
: doVAR        ( -- a )  R> ;
```

Pop return stack to data stack

```
VARIABLE UP    ( -- a, Pointer to the user area.)


: doUSER       ( -- a, Run time routine for user variables.)
    R> @               \ retrieve user area offset
    UP @ + ;           \ add to user area base addr


: doVOC        ( -- )      R> CONTEXT ! ;


: FORTH        ( -- )      doVOC [ 0 , 0 ,


: doUSER       ( -- a )    R> @ UP @ + ;
```

all confusing

eForth provides many functions in the vectored form to allow the behavior the these functions to be changed dynamically at run time. A vectored function stores a code address in a user variable. @EXECUTE is used to execute the function, given the address of the user variable. Following is the list of user variables defined in eForth:

```
SP0       ( -- a, pointer to bottom of the data stack.)
RP0       ( -- a, pointer to bottom of the return stack.)
'?KEY     ( -- a, execution vector of ?KEY.  Default to ?rx.)
'EMIT     ( -- a, execution vector of EMIT.  Default to tx!)
'EXPECT   ( -- a, execution vector of EXPECT. Default to 'accept'.)
'TAP      ( -- a, execution vector of TAP.  Defulat the kTAP.)
'ECHO     ( -- a, execution vector of ECHO.  Default to tx!.)
'PROMPT   ( -- a, execution vector of PROMPT.  Default to '.ok'.)
BASE      ( -- a,.radix base for numeric I/O.  Default to 10.)
Tmp       ( -- a, a temporary storage location used in parse and
                  find.)
SPAN      ( -- a, hold character count received by EXPECT.)
>IN       ( -- a, hold the character pointer
                  while parsing input stream.)
#TIB      ( -- a, hold the current count and address
                  of the terminal input buffer.
                  Terminal Input Buffer used one cell after #TIB.)
CSP       ( -- a, hold the stack pointer for error checking.)
```

```
'EVAL    ( -- a, execution vector of EVAL. Default to EVAL.)
'NUMBER  ( -- a, address of number conversion.
                   Default to NUMBER?.)
HLD    ( -- a, hold a pointer in building a numeric output string.)
HANDLER ( -- a, hold the return stack pointer for error handling.)
CONTEXT (  --  a,  a  area  to  specify  vocabulary  search  order.
                   Default to FORTH.
                   Vocabulary stack, 8 cells follwing CONTEXT.)
CURRENT ( -- a, point to the vocabulary to be extended.
                   Default to FORTH.
                   Vocabulary link uses one cell after CURRENT.)
CP       ( -- a, point to the top of the code dictionary.)
NP       ( -- a, point to the bottom of the name dictionary.)
LAST     ( -- a, point to the last name in the name dictionary.)
```

3.2 Common Functions

This group of Forth words are commonly used in writing Forth applications. They are coded in high level to enhance the portability of eForth. In most Forth implementations, they are coded in machine language to increase the execute speed. After an eForth system is ported to a new CPU, this word set should be recoded in assembly to improve the run time performance of the system.

> ?DUP,   ROT,   2DROP,   and   2DUP

are stack operators supplementing the four classic stack operators

> DUP,   SWAP,   OVER,   and   DROP.

ROT is unique in that it accesses the third item on the data stack. All other stack operators can only access one or two stack items. In Forth programming, it is generally accepted that one should not try to access stack items deeper than the third item. When you have to access deeper into the data stack, it is a good time to re-evaluate your algorithm. Most often, you can avoid this situation by factoring your code into smaller parts which do not reach so deep.

+, - and D+ are simple extensions from the primitive word UM+. It is interesting to see how the more commonly used arithmetic operators are derived. + is UM+ with the carry discarded. NOT returns the ones compliment of a number and NEGATE returns the two's compliment. Because UM+ preserves the carry, it can be used to form multiple precision operators like D+.

Later we will see how UM+ is used to do multiplication and division.

```
: ?DUP      ( w -- w w | 0 )           DUP IF DUP THEN ;
: ROT       ( w1 w2 w3 -- w2 w3 w1 )   >R SWAP R> SWAP ;
: 2DROP     ( w w  -- )                DROP DROP ;
: 2DUP      ( w1 w2 -- w1 w2 w1 w2 )   OVER OVER ;
: +         ( w w -- w )               UM+ DROP ;
: NOT       ( w -- w )                 -1 XOR ;
: NEGATE    ( n -- -n )                NOT 1 + ;
: DNEGATE   ( d -- -d )                NOT >R NOT 1 UM+ R> + ;
: D+        ( d d -- d )               >R SWAP >R UM+ R> R> + + ;
: -         ( w w -- w )               NEGATE + ;
: ABS       ( n -- +n )                DUP 0< IF NEGATE THEN ;
```

3.3 Comparison

The primitive comparison word in eForth is **?branch** and **0<**. However, ?branch is at such a low level that it can not be readily used in high level Forth code. ?branch is secretly compiled into the high level Forth words by IF as an address literal. For all intentions and purposes, we can consider IF the equivalent of ?branch.

When IF is encountered, the top item on the data stack is considered a logic flag. If it is true (non-zero), the execution continues until ELSE, then jump to THEN, or to THEN directly if there is no ELSE clause.

The following logic words are constructed using the IF...ELSE...THEN structure with 0< and XOR. XOR is used as 'not equal' operator, because if the top two items on the data stack are not equal, the XOR operator will return a non-zero number, which is considered to be 'true'.

U< is used to compared two unsigned numbers. This operator is very important, especially in comparing addresses, as we assume that the addresses are unsigned numbers pointing to unique memory locations. The arithmetic comparison operator < cannot be used to determine whether one address is higher or lower than the other. Using < for address comparison had been the single cause of many failures in the annals of Forth.

MAX retains the larger of the top two items on the data stack. Both numbers are assumed to be signed integers.

MIN retains the smaller of the top two items on the data stack. Both numbers are assumed to be signed integers.

WITHIN checks whether the third item on the data stack is within the range as specified by the top two numbers on the data stack. The range is inclusive as to the lower limit and exclusive to the upper limit. If the third item is within range, a true flag is returned on the data stack. Otherwise, a false flag is returned. All numbers are assumed to be unsigned integers.

```
: =      ( w w -- t )   XOR IF 0 EXIT THEN -1 ;

: U<     ( u u -- t ) 2DUP XOR 0< IF SWAP DROP 0< EXIT THEN - 0< ;

: <      ( n n -- t ) 2DUP XOR 0< IF      DROP 0< EXIT THEN - 0< ;

: MAX  ( n n -- n ) 2DUP      < IF SWAP THEN DROP ;

: MIN  ( n n -- n ) 2DUP SWAP < IF SWAP THEN DROP ;

: WITHIN ( u ul uh -- t )   \ ul <= u < uh   OVER - >R - R> U< ;
```

3.4 Divide

This group of words provide a variety of multiplication and division functions. The most interesting feature of this word set is that they are all based on the primitive UM+ operator in the kernel. Building this word set in high level has the penalty that all math operations will be slow.

However, since eForth needs these functions only in numeric I/O conversions, the performance of eForth itself is not substantially affected by them. Nevertheless, if an application requires lots of numeric computations, a few critical words in this word set should be recoded in assembly. The primary candidates for optimization are UM/MOD and UM*, because all other multiply and divide operators are derived from these two words.

UM/MOD and UM* are the most complicated and comprehensive division and multiplication operators. Once they are coded, all other division and multiplication operators can be derived easily. It has been a tradition in Forth coding that one solves the most difficult problem first, and all other problems are solved by themselves.

UM/MOD divides an unsigned double integer by an unsigned signal integer. It returns the unsigned remainder and unsigned quotient on the data stack.

M/MOD divides a signed double integer by a signed signal integer. It returns the signed remainder and signed quotient on the data stack. The signed division is floored towards negative infinity.

/MOD divides a signed single integer by a signed integer. It returns the signed remainder and quotient. MOD is similar to /MOD, except that only the signed remainder is returned. / is also similar to /MOD, except that only the signed quotient is returned.

In most advanced microprocessors like 8086, all these division operations can be performed by the CPU as native machine instructions. The user can take advantage of these machine instructions by recoding these Forth words in machine code.

```
: UM/MOD ( ud u -- ur uq )
    2DUP U<
    IF NEGATE   15
      FOR >R DUP UM+ >R >R DUP UM+ R> + DUP
        R> R@ SWAP >R UM+   R> OR
      IF >R DROP 1 + R> ELSE DROP THEN R>
      NEXT DROP SWAP EXIT
    THEN DROP 2DROP   -1 DUP ;

: M/MOD ( d n -- r q ) \ floored division
    DUP 0<   DUP >R
    IF NEGATE >R DNEGATE R>
    THEN >R DUP 0< IF R@ + THEN R> UM/MOD R>
    IF SWAP NEGATE SWAP THEN ;

: /MOD ( n n -- r q ) OVER 0< SWAP M/MOD ;

: MOD   ( n n -- r ) /MOD DROP ;

: /     ( n n -- q ) /MOD SWAP DROP ;
```

3.5 Multiply

UM* is the most complicated multiplication operation. Once it is coded, all other multiplication words can be derived from it.

UM* multiplies two unsigned single integers and returns the unsigned double integer product on the data stack. M* multiplies two signed single integers and returns the signed double integer product on the data stack. * multiplies two signed single integers and returns the signed single integer product on the data stack.

Again, advanced CPU's generally have these multiplication operations as native machine instructions. The user should take advantage of these resources to enhance the eForth system.

Forth is very close to the machine language that it generally only handles integer numbers. There are floating point extensions on many more sophisticated Forth systems, but they are more exceptions than rules.

The reason that Forth has traditionally been an integer language is that integers are handled faster and more efficiently in the computers, and most technical problems can be solved satisfactorily using integers only. A 16-bit integer has the dynamic range of 110 dB which is far more than enough for most engineering problems.

The precision of a 16-bit integer representation is limited to one part in 65535, which could be inadequate for small numbers. However, the precision can be greatly improved by scaling; i.e., taking the ratio of two integers. It was demonstrated that pi, or any other irrational numbers, can be represented accurately to 1 part in 100,000,000 by a ratio of two 16-bit integers.

The scaling operators */MOD and */ are useful in scaling number n1 by the ratio of n2/n3. When n2 and n3 are properly chosen, the scaling operation can preserve precision similar to the floating point operations at a much higher speed. Notice also that in these scaling operations, the intermediate product of n1 and n2 is a double precision integer so that the precision of scaling is maintained.

*/MOD multiplies the signed integers n1 and n2, and then divides the double integer product by n3. It in fact is ratioing n1 by n2/n3. It returns both the remainder and the quotient. */ is similar to */MOD except that it only returns the quotient.

```
: UM*  ( u u -- ud )
    0 SWAP ( u1 0 u2 ) 15
    FOR DUP UM+ >R >R DUP UM+ R> + R>
    IF >R OVER UM+ R> + THEN
    NEXT ROT DROP ;

: *      ( n n -- n ) UM* DROP ;

: M*     ( n n -- d )
             2DUP XOR 0< >R  ABS SWAP ABS UM*  R>
             IF DNEGATE THEN ;

: */MOD ( n n n -- r q ) >R M* R> M/MOD ;

: */     ( n n n -- q ) */MOD SWAP DROP ;
```

3.6 Memory Alignment

The most serious problem in porting system from one computer to another is that different computers have different sizes for their addresses and data. We generally classify computers as 8, 16, 32, ... , bit machines, because they operate on data of these various sizes.

It is thus difficult to port a single programming model as eForth to all these computers. In eForth, a set of memory alignment words helps to make it easier to port the eForth model to different machines. We assume that the target computer can address it memory in 8 bit chunks (bytes).

The natural width of data best handled by the computer is thus a multiple of bytes. A unit of such data is a cell. An 16 bit machine handles data in 2 byte cells, and a 32 bit machine handles data in 4 byte cells.

CELL+ increments the memory address by the cell size in bytes, and **CELL-** decrements the memory address by the cell size. **CELLS** multiplies the cell number on the stack by the cell size in bytes. These words are very useful in converting a cell offset into a byte offset, in order to access integers in a data array.

ALIGNED converts an address on the stack to the next cell boundary, to help accessing memory by cells.

The blank character (ASCII 32) is special in eForth because it is the most often used character to delimit words in the input stream and the most often used character to format the output strings. It is used so often that it is advantageous to define an unique word for it. BL simply returns the number 32 on the data stack.

>CHAR is very important in converting a non-printable character to a harmless 'underscare' character (ASCII 95). As eForth is designed to communicate with a host computer through the serial I/O device, it is important that eForth will not emit control characters to the host and causes unexpected behavior on the host computer. >CHAR thus filters the characters before they are sent out by EMIT.

DEPTH returns the number of items currently on the data stack to the top of the stack. PICK takes a number n off the data stack and replaces it with the n'th item on the data stack. The number n is 0-based; i.e., the top item is number 0, the next item is number 1, etc. Therefore, 0 PICK is equivalent to DUP, and 1 PICK is equivalent to OVER.

```
: CELL-    ( a -- a )  -2 + ;
: CELL+    ( a -- a )   2 + ;
: CELLS    ( n -- n )   2 * ;

: ALIGNED ( b -- a )
      DUP 0 2 UM/MOD DROP DUP
      IF 2 SWAP - THEN + ;

: BL       ( -- 32 )   32 ;

: >CHAR    ( c -- c )
      $7F AND DUP 127 BL WITHIN IF DROP 95 THEN ;

: DEPTH    ( -- n )  SP@ SP0 @ SWAP - 2 / ;

: PICK     ( +n -- w )  1 + CELLS SP@ + @ ;
```

3.7 Memory Access

Here are three useful memory operators. +! increments the contents of a memory location by an integer on the stack. 2! and 2@ store and fetch double integers to and from memory.

There are three buffer areas used often in the eForth system. HERE returns the address of the first free location above the code dictionary, where new words are compiled. PAD returns the address of the text buffer where numbers are constructed, and text strings are stored temporarily. TIB is the terminal input buffer where input text string is held.

@EXECUTE is a special word supporting the vectored execution words in eForth. It takes the word address stored in a memory location and executes the word. It is used extensively to execute the vectored words in the user area.

A memory array is generally specified by a starting address and its length in bytes. In a string, the first byte is a count byte, specifying the number of bytes in the following string. This is called a counted string. String literals in the colon definitions and the name strings in the name dictionary are all represented by counted strings. Following are special words which handles memory arrays and strings.

COUNT converts a string array address to the address-length representation of a counted string. CMOVE copies a memory array from one location to another. FILL fills a memory array with the same byte.

Arrays and strings are generally specified by the address of the first byte in the array or string, and the byte length. This specification of course is the consequence that the memory is byte addressable. In a CPU which address memory in cells, these words must be defined in terms of an artificial byte space.

-TRAILING removes the trailing white space characters from the end of a string. White space characters include all the non-printable characters below ASCII 32. This word allows eForth to process text lines in files downloaded from a host computer. It conveniently eliminates carriage-returns, life-feeds, tabs and spaces at the end of the text lines.

**PACK$** is an important string handling word used by the text interpreter. It copies a text string from on location to another. In the target area, the string is converted to a counted string by adding a count byte before the text of the string. This word is used to build the name field of a new word at the bottom of the name dictionary. PACK$ is designed so that it can pack bytes into cells in a cell addressable machine.

A cheap way to implement eForth on a cell addressable machine is to equate cell addresses to byte addresses, and to store one byte in a cell. This scheme is workable, but very inefficient in the memory utilization. PACK$ is a tool which helps the implementor to bridge the gap.

```
: +!   ( n a -- )   SWAP OVER @ + SWAP ! ;

: 2!   ( d a -- )   SWAP OVER ! CELL+ ! ;

: 2@   ( a -- d )   DUP CELL+ @ SWAP @ ;
```

```
: COUNT   ( b -- b +n )   DUP 1 + SWAP C@ ;

: HERE    ( -- a )   CP @ ;

: PAD     ( -- a )   HERE 80 + ;

: TIB     ( -- a )   #TIB CELL+ @ ;

: @EXECUTE  ( a -- )   @ ?DUP IF EXECUTE THEN ;

: CMOVE ( b b u -- )
    FOR AFT >R DUP C@ R@ C! 1 + R> 1 + THEN NEXT 2DROP ;

: FILL ( b u c -- )
    SWAP FOR SWAP AFT 2DUP C! 1 + THEN NEXT 2DROP ;

: -TRAILING ( b u -- b u )
    FOR AFT BL OVER R@ + C@ <
      IF R> 1 + EXIT THEN THEN
    NEXT 0 ;

: PACK$ ( b u a -- a )                       \ null fill
    ALIGNED  DUP >R OVER
    DUP 0 2 UM/MOD DROP
    - OVER +  0 SWAP !  2DUP C!  1 + SWAP CMOVE  R> ;
```

4.0 Text Interpreter

The text interpreter is also called the outer interpreter in Forth. It is functionally equivalent to an operating system in a conventional computer. It accepts command similar to English entered by a user and carries out the tasks specified by the commands. As an operating system, the text interpreter must be complicated, because of all the things it has to do.

However, because Forth employs very simple syntax rules, and has very simple internal structures, the Forth text interpreter is much simpler that conventional operating systems. It is simple enough that we can discuss it completely in a single chapter, admitted that this is a long chapter.

Let us summarize what a text interpreter must do:

> **Accept text input from a terminal**
> **Parse out commands from input text**
> **Search dictionary**
> **Execute commands**
> **Translate numbers into binary**
> **Display numbers in text form**
> **Handle errors gracefully**

Forth allows us to build and integrate these required functions gradually in modules. All the modules finally fall into their places in the word QUIT, which is the text interpreter itself.

You might want to look up the code of QUIT first and see how the modules fit together. A good feeling about the big picture will help you in the study of the smaller modules. Nevertheless, we will doggedly follow the loading order of the source code, and hope that you will not get lost too far in the progress.

4.1 Numeric Output

Forth is interesting in its special capabilities in handling numbers across the man-machine interface. It recognizes that the machine and the human prefer very different representations of numbers. The machine prefers the binary representation, but the human prefers decimal Arabic digital representations.

However, depending on circumstances, the human may want numbers to be represented in other radices, like hexadecimal, octal, and sometimes binary.

Forth solves this problem of internal (machine) versus external (human) number representations by insisting that all numbers are represented in the binary form in the CPU and in memory. Only when numbers are imported or exported for human consumption are they converted to the external ASCII representation. The radix of external representation is controlled by the radix value stored in the user variable BASE.

Since BASE is a user variable, the user can select any reasonable radix for entering numbers into the computer and format ting numbers to be shown to the user. Most programming languages can handle a small set of radices, like decimal, octal, hexadecimal and binary. DIGIT converts an integer to a digit. EXTRACT extracts the least significan digit from a number n. n is divided by the radix in BASE and returned on the stack.

The output number string is built below the PAD buffer. The least significant digit is extracted from the integer on the top of the data stack by dividing it by the current radix in BASE. The digit thus extracted are added to the output string backwards from PAD to the low memory. The conversion is terminated when the integer is divided to zero. The address and length of the number string are made available by #> for outputting.

An output number conversion is initiated by <# and terminated by #>. Between them, # converts one digit at a time, #S converts all the digits, while HOLD and SIGN inserts special characters into the string under construction. This set of words is very versatile and can handle many different output formats.

```
: DIGIT     ( u -- c )   9 OVER < 7 AND + 48 + ;

: EXTRACT ( n base -- n c )  0 SWAP UM/MOD SWAP DIGIT ;

: <#        ( -- )        PAD HLD ! ;

: HOLD      ( c -- )      HLD @ 1 - DUP HLD ! C! ;

: #         ( u -- u )    BASE @ EXTRACT HOLD ;

: #S        ( u -- 0 )    BEGIN # DUP WHILE REPEAT ;

: SIGN      ( n -- )      0< IF 45 HOLD THEN ;

: #>        ( w -- b u )  DROP HLD @ PAD OVER - ;

: str       ( n -- b u )  DUP >R ABS <# #S R> SIGN #> ;

: HEX       ( -- )        16 BASE ! ;
: DECIMAL ( -- )          10 BASE ! ;
```

4.2 Number Output

With the number formatting word set as shown above, one can format
numbers for output in any form desired. The free output format is a
number string preceded by a single space. The fix column format
displays a number right-justified in a column of pre-determined
width. The words ., U., and ? use the free format. The words .R and
U.R use the fixed format.

```
: str    ( n -- b u )
            ( Convert a signed integer to a numeric string.)
         DUP >R    ( save a copy for sign)
         ABS       ( use absolute of n)
         <# #S     ( convert all digits)
         R> SIGN   ( add sign from n)
         #> ;      ( return number string addr and length)

: HEX   ( -- )
            ( Use radix 16 as base for numeric conversions.)
         16 BASE ! ;

: DECIMAL  ( -- )
            ( Use radix 10 as base for numeric conversions.)
         10 BASE ! ;

: .R    ( n +n -- )
         ( Display an integer in a field of n columns, )
         ( right justified.)
         >R str              ( convert n to a number string)
         R> OVER - SPACES    ( print leading spaces)
         TYPE ;              ( print number in +n column format)

: U.R   ( u +n -- )
         ( Display an unsigned integer in n column,
         ( right justified.)
         >R                  ( save column number)
```

```
        <# #S #> R>    ( convert unsigned number)
        OVER - SPACES ( print leading spaces)
        TYPE ;         ( print number in +n columns)

: U.   ( u -- )
        ( Display an unsigned integer in free format.)
        <# #S #>     ( convert unsigned number)
         SPACE        ( print one leading space)
         TYPE ;       ( print number)

: .    ( w -- )
        ( Display an integer in free format,
        ( preceeded by a space.)
        BASE @ 10 XOR         ( if not in decimal mode)
        IF U. EXIT THEN       ( print unsigned number)
        str SPACE TYPE ;      ( print signed number if decimal)

: ?    ( a -- )
        ( Display the contents in a memory cell.)
        @ . ;       ( very simple but useful command)
```

4.3 Numeric Input

The Forth text interpreter also handles the number input to the system. It parses words out of the input stream and try to execute the words in sequence. When the text interpreter encounters a word, which is not the name of a word in the dictionary, it then assumes that the word must be a number and attempts to convert the ASCII string to a number according to the current radix.

When the text interpreter succeeds in converting the string to a number, the number is pushed on the data stack for future use if the text interpreter is in the interpreting mode. If it is in the compiling mode, the text interpreter will compile the number to the code dictionary as an integer literal so that when the word under construction is later executed, this literal integer will be pushed on the data stack.

If the text interpreter fails to convert the word to a number, there is an error condition which will cause the text interpreter to abort, posting an error message to the user, and then wait for the user's next line of commands.

Only two words are needed in eForth to handle input of single precision integer numbers.

DIGIT? converts a digit to its numeric value according to the current base, and NUMBER? converts a number string to a single integer. NUMBER? is vectored through 'NUMBER to convert numbers.

NUMBER? converts a string of digits to a single integer. If the first character is a $ sign, the number is assumed to be in hexadecimal. Otherwise, the number will be converted using the radix value stored in BASE. For negative numbers, the first character should be a - sign. No other characters are allowed in the string.

If a non-digit character is encountered, the address of the string and a false flag are returned. Successful conversion returns the integer value and a true flag. If the number is larger than $2^{**}n$, where n is the bit width of the single integer, only the modulus to $2^{**}n$ will be kept.

```
: DIGIT?      ( c base -- u t )
    >R 48 - 9 OVER <
    IF 7 - DUP 10 < OR THEN DUP R> U< ;

: NUMBER?  ( a -- n T | a F )
    BASE @ >R   0 OVER COUNT           ( a 0 b n)
    OVER C@ 36 =
    IF HEX SWAP 1 + SWAP 1 - THEN   ( a 0 b' n')
    OVER C@ 45 = >R                 ( a 0 b n)
    SWAP R@ - SWAP R@ + ( a 0 b" n") ?DUP
    IF 1 - ( a 0 b n)
      FOR DUP >R C@ BASE @ DIGIT?
        WHILE SWAP BASE @ * +   R> 1 +
      NEXT DROP R@ ( b ?sign) IF NEGATE THEN SWAP
        ELSE R> R> ( b index) 2DROP ( digit number) 2DROP 0
        THEN DUP
    THEN R> ( n ?sign) 2DROP R> BASE ! ;
```

4.4 Basic I/O

The eForth system assumes that the system will communicate with its environment only through a serial I/O interface. To support the serial I/O, only three words are needed:

?KEY returns a false flag if no character is pending on the receiver. If a character is received, the character and a true flag are returned. This word is more powerful than that usually defined in most Forth systems because it consolidate the functionality of KEY into ?KEY. It simplifies the coding of the machine dependent I/O interface.

KEY will execute ?KEY continually until a valid character is received and the character is returned.

EMIT sends a character out throughout the transmit line.
?KEY and EMIT are vectored through '?KEY and 'EMIT, so that their function can be changed dynamically at run time. Normally, ?KEY executes ?RX and EMIT executes TX!. ?RX and TX! are machine dependent kernel words. Vectoring the I/O words allows the eForth system to changes its I/O channels dynamically and still uses all the existing tools to handle input and output transactions.

All I/O words are derived from ?KEY, KEY and EMIT. The following set defined in eForth is particularly useful in normal programming: **SPACE** outputs a blank space character. SPACES output n blank space characters. CR outputs a carriage-return and a line-feed. PACE outputs an ASCII 11 character to acknowledge lines received during file downloading.

NUF? returns a false flag if no character is pending in the input buffer. After receiving a character, pause and wait for another character. If this character is CR, return a true flag; otherwise, return false. This word is very useful in user interruptable routines.

TYPE outputs n characters from a string in memory.

With the number formatting word set as shown above, one can format numbers for output in any form desired. The free output format is a number string preceded by a single space. The fix column format displays a number right-justified in a column of pre-determined width. The words ., U., and ? use the free format. The words .R and U.R use the fix format.

String literals are data structures compiled in colon definitions, in-line with the words. A string literal must start with a string word which knows how to handle the following string at the run time. Let us show two examples of the string literals:

```
: xxx   ...    " A compiled string"   ...   ;
: yyy   ...   ." An output string"   ...   ;
```

In xxx, " is an immediate word which compiles the following string as a string literal preceded by a special word $"|. When $"| is executed at the run time, it returns the address of this string on the data stack. In yyy, ." compiles a string literal preceded by another word ."|, which prints the compiled string to the output device.

Both $"| and ."| use the word do$, which retrieve the address of a string stored as the second item on the return stack. do$ is a bit difficult to understand, because the starting address of the following string is the second item on the return stack. This address is pushed on the data stack so that the string can be accessed.

This address must be changed so that the address interpreter will return to the word right after the compiled string. This address will allow the address interpreter to skip over the string literal and continue to execute the word list as intended.

```
: ?KEY      ( -- c T  | F )  '?KEY @EXECUTE  ;
: KEY       ( -- c )   BEGIN ?KEY UNTIL ;
: EMIT      ( c -- )    'EMIT @EXECUTE  ;


: NUF?      ( -- f )   ?KEY DUP IF 2DROP KEY 13 = THEN ;

: PACE      ( -- )     11  EMIT ;
: SPACE     ( -- )     BL EMIT ;

: CHARS     ( +n c -- )    \ ???ANS conflict
         SWAP   0 MAX FOR AFT DUP EMIT THEN NEXT DROP ;

: SPACES    ( +n -- )    BL CHARS ;

: TYPE      ( b u -- )  FOR AFT DUP C@ EMIT
         1 + THEN NEXT DROP ;

: CR        ( -- )   13 EMIT 10 EMIT ;

: do$       ( -- a )
         R> R@ R> COUNT + ALIGNED >R SWAP >R ;

: $"|       ( -- a )   do$ ;

: ."|       ( -- )     do$ COUNT TYPE ; COMPILE-ONLY


: .R        ( n +n -- )   >R  str R> OVER -
            SPACES TYPE ;

: U.R       ( u +n -- )   >R <# #S #> R> OVER -
       SPACES TYPE ;
```

```
: U.    ( u -- )  <# #S #> SPACE TYPE ;

: .     ( n -- )  BASE @ 10 XOR IF U. EXIT THEN
   str SPACE TYPE ;

: ?     ( a -- )  @ . ;
```

4.5 Parsing

Parsing is always thought of as a very advanced topic in computer sciences. However, because Forth uses very simple syntax rules, parsing is easy. Forth source code consists of words, which are ASCII strings separated by spaces and other white space characters like tabs, carriage returns, and line feeds.

The text interpreter scans the source code, isolates words and interprets them in sequence. After a word is parsed out of the input text stream, the text interpreter will 'interpret' it--execute it if it is a word, compile it if the text interpreter is in the compiling mode, and convert it to a number if the word is not a Forth word.

PARSE scans the source string in the terminal input buffer from where >IN points to till the end of the buffer, for a word delimited by character c. It returns the address and length of the word parsed out. PARSE calls 'parse' to do the detailed works. PARSE is used to implement many specialized parsing words to perform different source code handling functions. These words, including (, \, CHAR, WORD, and WORD are discussed in the next section.

'parse' (b1 u1 c -- b2 u2 n) is the elementary command to do text parsing. From the source string starting at b1 and of u1 characters long, parse out the first word delimited by character c. Return the address b2 and length u2 of the word just parsed out and the difference n between b1 and b2. Leading delimiters are skipped over. 'parse' is used by PARSE.

. (types the following string till the next). It is used to output text to the terminal. (ignores the following string till the next). It is used to place comments in source text. \ ignores all characters till end of input buffer. It is used to insert comment lines in text.

CHAR parses the next word but only return the first character in this word. Get an ASCII character from the input stream. WORD parses out the next word delimited by the ASCII character c.

Copy the word to the top of the code dictionary and return the address of this counted string. WORD parses the next word from the input buffer and copy the counted string to the top of the name dictionary. Return the address of this counted string.

```
: parse     ( b u c -- b u delta ; <string> )
  tmp !  OVER >R  DUP \ b u u
  IF 1 -   tmp @ BL =
    IF \ b u' \ 'skip'
      FOR BL OVER C@ - 0< NOT  WHILE 1 +
      NEXT ( b) R> DROP 0 DUP EXIT \ all delim
        THEN  R>
    THEN OVER SWAP \ b' b' u' \ 'scan'
    FOR tmp @ OVER C@ -  tmp @ BL =
      IF 0< THEN WHILE 1 +
    NEXT DUP >R  ELSE R> DROP DUP 1 + >R
               THEN OVER -  R>  R> - EXIT
  THEN ( b u) OVER R> - ;

: PARSE     ( c -- b u ; <string> )
  >R   TIB >IN @ +  #TIB @ >IN @ -  R> parse >IN +! ;
```

```
: .(      ( -- )   41 PARSE TYPE ; IMMEDIATE

: (       ( -- )   41 PARSE 2DROP ; IMMEDIATE

: \       ( -- )   #TIB @ >IN ! ; IMMEDIATE

: CHAR    ( -- c ) BL PARSE DROP C@ ;

: TOKEN   ( -- a ; <string> )
    BL PARSE 31 MIN NP @ OVER - CELL- PACK$ ;

: WORD    ( c -- a ; <string> ) PARSE HERE PACK$ ;
```

4.6 Dictionary Search

In eForth, headers of word definitions are linked into a name dictionary which is separated from the code dictionary. A header contains three fields: a word field holding the code address of the word, a link field holding the name field address of the previous header and a name field holding the name as a counted string.

The name dictionary is a list linked through the link fields and the name fields. The basic searching function is performed by the word 'find'. 'find' follows the linked list of names to find a name which matches a text string and returns the address of the executable word and the name field address, if a match is found.

eForth allows multiple vocabularies in the name dictionary. A dictionary can be divided into a number of independently linked sublists through some hashing mechanism. A sublist is called a vocabulary. Although eForth itself contains only one vocabulary, it has the provision to build many vocabularies and allows many vocabularies to be searched in a prioritized order. The CONTEXT array in the user area has 8 cells and allows up to 8 vocabularies to be searched in sequence. A null entry in the CONTEXT array terminates the vocabulary search.

find (a va -- ca na, a F) A counted string at a is the name of a word to be looked up in the dictionary. The last name field address of the vocabulary is stored in location va. If the string is found, both the word (code address) and the name field address are returned. If the string is not the name a word, the string address and a false flag are returned.

To locate a word, one could follow the linked list and compare the names of defined words to the string to be searched. If the string matches the name of a word in the name dictionary, the word and the address of the name field are returned.

If the string is not a defined word, the search will lead to either a null link or a null name field. In either case, the search will be terminated, and a false flag returned. The false flag thus indicates that the word searched is not in this vocabulary.

'find' runs through the name dictionary very quickly because it first compares the length and the first character in the name field as a cell. In most cases of mismatch, this comparison would fail, and the next name can be reached through the link field.

If the first two characters match, then SAME? is invoked to compare the rest of the name field, one cell at a time. Since both the target text string and the name field are null filled to the cell boundary, the comparison can be performed quickly across the entire name field without worrying about the end conditions.

NAME? (a -- ca na, a F) Search all the vocabularies in the CONTEXT array for a name at address a. Return the word and a name address if a matched word is found. Otherwise, return the string address and a false flag. The CONTEXT array can hold up to 8 vocabulary links.

However, a 0 which is not a valid vocabulary link in this array will terminate the searching. Changing the vocabulary links in this array and the order of these links will alter the searching order and hence the searching priority among the vocabularies.

```
: NAME> ( a -- xt ) CELL- CELL- @ ;

: SAME? ( a a u -- a a f \ -0+ )
    FOR AFT OVER R@ CELLS + @
            OVER R@ CELLS + @ - ?DUP
    IF R> DROP EXIT THEN THEN
  NEXT 0 ;

: find ( a va -- xt na | a F )
  SWAP                 \ va a
  DUP C@ 2 / tmp !  \ va a  \ get cell count
  DUP @ >R             \ va a  \ count byte & 1st char
  CELL+ SWAP           \ a' va
  BEGIN @ DUP          \ a' na na
   IF DUP @ [ =MASK ] LITERAL AND  R@ XOR \ ignore lexicon bits
      IF CELL+ -1 ELSE CELL+ tmp @ SAME? THEN
   ELSE R> DROP EXIT
   THEN
  WHILE CELL- CELL- \ a' la
  REPEAT R> DROP SWAP DROP CELL-  DUP NAME> SWAP ;

: NAME? ( a -- xt na | a F )
  CONTEXT  DUP 2@ XOR IF CELL- THEN >R \ context<>also
  BEGIN R>  CELL+  DUP >R  @  ?DUP
  WHILE find  ?DUP
  UNTIL R> DROP EXIT THEN R> DROP  0 ;
```

4.7 Terminal

The text interpreter interprets source text stored in the terminal input buffer. To process characters from the input device, we need three special words to deal with backspaces and carriage return from the input device:

kTAP processes a character c received from terminal. b1 is the starting address of the input buffer. b2 is the end of the input buffer. b3 is the currently available address in the input buffer. c is normally stored into b3, which is bumped by 1 and becomes b5. In this case, b4 is the same as b2. If c is a carriage-return, echo a space and make b4=b5=b3. If c is a back-space, erase the last character and make b4=b2, b5=b3-1. TAP echoes c to output device, store c in b3, and bump b3.

^H processes the back-space character. Erase the last character and decrement b3. If b3=b1, do nothing because you cannot backup beyond the beginning of the input buffer.

QUERY is the word which accepts text input, up to 80 characters, from the input device and copies the text characters to the terminal input buffer. It also prepares the terminal input buffer for parsing by setting #TIB to the character count and clearing >IN.

EXPECT accepts u characters to a memory buffer starting at b. The input is terminated upon receiving a carriage-return. The number of characters actually received is stored in SPAN. EXPECT is called by QUERY to put characters into the terminal input buffer. However, EXPECT is useful by itself because one can use it to place input text anywhere in the memory. QUERY and EXPECT are the two words most useful in accepting text from the terminal.

'accept' accepts u1 characters to b. u2 returned is the actual count of characters received.

```
: ^H ( b b b -- b b b )        \ backspace
  >R OVER R> SWAP OVER XOR
    IF  8 'ECHO @EXECUTE
       32 'ECHO @EXECUTE        \ distructive
        8 'ECHO @EXECUTE        \ backspace
    THEN ;
: TAP ( bot eot cur c -- bot eot cur )
    DUP 'ECHO @EXECUTE OVER C! 1 + ;

: kTAP ( bot eot cur c -- bot eot cur )
    DUP 13 XOR
    IF 8 XOR IF BL TAP ELSE ^H THEN EXIT
    THEN DROP SWAP DROP DUP ;

: accept ( b u -- b u )
    OVER + OVER
    BEGIN 2DUP XOR
    WHILE  KEY  DUP BL -  95 U<
      IF TAP ELSE 'TAP @EXECUTE THEN
    REPEAT DROP  OVER - ;

: EXPECT ( b u -- )  EXPECT @EXECUTE SPAN ! DROP ;

: QUERY ( -- )
   TIB 80 'EXPECT @EXECUTE #TIB !  DROP 0 >IN ! ;
```

4.8 Error Handling

This error handling mechanism was first developed by Mitch Bradley in his ForthMacs and then adopted by the ANS Forth Standard. It is very simple yet very powerful in customizing system responses to many different error conditions.

CATCH sets up a local error frame and execute the word referenced by the execution word ca. It returns a non-zero error code or a zero if no error occurred. As the assigned word at ca is executing, any error condition will execute THROW, which pushes an error code on the data stack, restore the return stack to the state before CATCH was executed, and execute the error handler stored in HANDLER. Since the error handler frame is saved on the return stack, many layers of safety nets can be laid down nested.

CATCH pushes SP and HANDLER on the return stack, saves RP in HANDLER, and then execute the word at ca. If no error occurred, HANDLER and SP are restored from the return stack and a 0 is pushed on the data stack.

THROW throws the system back to CATCH so that the error condition can be processed. CATCH is backtracked by restoring the return stack from the pointer stored in HANDLER and popping the old handler and SP off the error frame on the return stack.

```
: CATCH ( ca -- err#/0 )
        ( Execute word at ca and set up an error frame for it.)
    SP@ >R       ( save current stack pointer on return stack )
    HANDLER @ >R  ( save the handler pointer on return stack )
   RP@ HANDLER !  ( save the handler frame pointer in HANDLER )
```

```
       ( ca )  EXECUTE
  ( execute the assigned word over this safety net )
     R> HANDLER !     ( normal return from the executed word )
                      ( restore HANDLER from the return stack )
     R> DROP          ( discard the saved data stack pointer )
     0 ;              ( push a no-error flag on data stack )


 : THROW ( err# -- err# )
           ( Reset system to current local error frame)
           ( an update error flag.)
        HANDLER @ RP!    ( expose latest error handler )
                         (  frame on return stack )
    R> HANDLER ! ( restore previously saved error handler frame )
    R> SWAP >R        ( retrieve the data stack pointer saved )
       SP!            ( restore the data stack )
       DROP
       R> ;              ( retrived err# )
```

**NULL$** is the address of a string with a zero count. This address is used by ABORT and abort" to terminate the interpreting of the current command line. QUIT tests the address reported by CATCH. If this address is NULL$, the termination is normal and no error message will be issued. If CATCH reports a different address, QUIT will display the contents of the string at that address.

ABORT" is used only within a definition to compile an inline packed string terminated by the " double quote character. At run-time, if the flag is false, execute the sequence of words following the string. Otherwise, the string is displayed on the current output device, and execution is then passed to an error handling routine.

You have to study the code in **QUIT** carefully with this section to get a better understanding of the CATCH-THROW error handling mechanism.

```
: CATCH  ( xt -- 0 | err# )

    SP@ >R   HANDLER @ >R   RP@ HANDLER !
    EXECUTE
    R> HANDLER !   R> DROP   0 ;

: THROW  ( err# -- err# )
        HANDLER @ RP!   R> HANDLER !   R> SWAP >R SP! DROP R> ;
        CREATE NULL$ 0 , $," coyote"

: ABORT  ( -- )      NULL$  THROW ;

: abort"  ( f -- )   IF do$ THROW THEN do$ DROP ;
```

Let's look at how the CATCH-THROW pair is used.
In QUIT, there is this an indefinite loop:

```
BEGIN   QUERY [ ' EVAL ] LITERAL   CATCH ?DUP   UNTIL
```

QUERY gets a line of text and CATCH causes EVAL to interpret the line. CATCH also sets up an error handling frame on the return stack and saves the return stack pointer in the user variable HANDLER. The error handling frame contains the current data stack pointer and the current contents in HANDLER.

If no error occurred during EVAL, the error frame is popped off the return stack and a false flag is returned on the data stack. ?DUP UNTIL will loop back to QUERY and the interpretive process will continue.

While EVAL interprets the text, any word which decided that it detects an error condition and needs attention, it will execute THROW. THROW restores the return stack from the pointer stored in HANDLER, making the error handling frame available.

THROW then restores HANDLER from the one saved in the error frame so that the error handling can be nested. The data stack pointer is also restored from the error frame. Now THROW passes the address of a error processing routine to the CATCH which built the error frame.

$INTERPRET, ?STACK and abort" pass string addresses to THROW. The strings contains appropriate error messages to be displayed by the text interpreter. In QUIT, the words between UNTIL and AGAIN deal with the error conditions and then re-initialize the text interpreter.

Here are some of the examples which generate error conditions:

```
: ABORT     NULL$ THROW ;

: abort"    IF do$ THROW THEN do$ DROP ;

: ?STACK    DEPTH 0< IF $" underflow" THROW THEN ;

: $INTERPRET    ... 'NUMBER @EXECUTE  IF EXIT THEN THROW ;
```

4.9 Text Interpreter

Text interpreter in Forth is like the operating system of a computer. It is the primary interface a user goes through to get the computer to do work. Since Forth uses very simple syntax rules--words are separated by spaces, the text interpreter is also very simple.

It accepts a line of text from the terminal, parses out a word delimited by spaces, locates the word of this word in the dictionary and then executes it. The process is repeated until the source text is exhausted. Then the text interpreter waits for another line of text and interprets it again. This cycle repeats until the user is exhausted and turns off the computer.

In eForth, the text interpreter is encoded in the word QUIT. QUIT contains an infinite loop which repeats the QUERY EVAL phrase. QUERY accepts a line of text from the terminal and copies the text into the Terminal Input Buffer (TIB). EVAL interprets the text one word at a time till the end of the text line.

One of the unique features in eForth is its error handling mechanism. While EVAL is interpreting a line of text, there could exist many error conditions: a word is not found in the dictionary and it is not a number, a compile-only word is accidentally executed interpretively, and the interpretive process may bee interrupted by the words ABORT or abort".

Wherever the error occurs, the text interpreter must be made aware of it so that it can recover gracefully from the error condition and continue on about the interpreting business.

$INTERPRET executes a word whose string address is on the stack. If the string is not a word, convert it to a number.

[activates the text interpreter by storing the execution address of $INTERPRET into the variable 'EVAL, which is executed in EVAL while the text interpreter is in the interpretive mode.

.OK prints the familiar 'ok' prompt after executing to the end of a line. 'ok' is printed only when the text interpreter is in the interpretive mode. While compiling, the prompt is suppressed.

?STACK checks for stack underflow. Abort if the stack depth is negative.

EVAL is the interpreter loop which parses words from the input stream and invokes whatever is in 'EVAL to handle that word, either execute it with $INTERPRET or compile it with $COMPILE.

```
: $INTERPRET     ( a -- )
     NAME?   ?DUP
     IF @ $40 AND
          ABORT" compile ONLY" EXECUTE EXIT
     THEN 'NUMBER @EXECUTE IF EXIT THEN THROW ;

: [     ( -- ) doLIT $INTERPRET 'EVAL ! ; IMMEDIATE

: .OK     ( -- )  doLIT $INTERPRET 'EVAL @ = IF ."  ok" THEN CR ;

: ?STACK     ( -- ) DEPTH 0< ABORT" underflow" ;

: EVAL     ( -- )
          BEGIN TOKEN DUP C@
            WHILE 'EVAL @EXECUTE ?STACK
            REPEAT DROP 'PROMPT @EXECUTE ;
```

4.10 Shell

Source code can be downloaded to eForth through the serial input device. The only precaution we have to take is that during file downloading, characters are not echoed back to the host computer. However, whenever an error occurred during downloading, it is more useful to resume echoing so that error messages can be displayed on the terminal.

It is also convenient to send special pacing characters to the host to tell the host that a line of source code was received and processed correctly. The following words configure the eForth I/O vectors to have the proper behavior in normal terminal interaction and also during file downloading:

FILE turns off character echoing. After one line of text is processed correctly, a pacing character ASCII 11 is sent to the host. If an error occurred, send an ESC (ASCII 26) character. An error will also restore the I/O vectors into the terminal mode. HAND resumes terminal interaction. Turn on character echoing and send normal prompt message after a line is processed correctly. CONSOLE initializes the serial I/O device for terminal interaction. ?KEY is vectored to ?RX and EMIT is vectored to TX!.

QUIT is the operating system, or a shell, of the eForth system. It is an infinite loop eForth will never get out. It uses QUERY to accept a line of commands from the terminal and then let EVAL parse out the words and execute them. After a line is processed, it displays 'ok' and wait for the next line of commands. When an error occurred during execution, it displays the command which caused the error with an error message. After the error is reported, it re-initializes the system using PRESET and comes back to receive the next line of commands. Because the behavior of EVAL can be changed by storing either $INTERPRET or $COMPILE into 'EVAL, QUIT exhibits the dual nature of a text interpreter and a compiler.

```
: PRESET ( -- )   SP0 @ SP!  TIB #TIB CELL+ ! ;

: xio    ( a a a -- )  \ reset  'EXPECT 'TAP  'ECHO 'PROMPT
      doLIT accept  ' EXPECT 2! 'ECHO 2! ; COMPILE-ONLY

: FILE   ( -- )
         doLIT PACE       doLIT DROP  doLIT kTAP xio ;

: HAND   ( -- )
         doLIT .OK        doLIT EMIT  [ kTAP  xio ;

  CREATE I/O     ' ?RX ,  ' TX! , \              defaults

: CONSOLE ( -- )  I/O 2@ '?KEY 2! HAND ;

: QUIT    ( -- )
       RP0 @ RP!
       BEGIN [COMPILE] [
           BEGIN QUERY doLIT EVAL CATCH ?DUP
           UNTIL 'PROMPT @ SWAP CONSOLE  NULL$ OVER XOR
               IF CR #TIB 2@ TYPE
                   CR >IN @ 94 CHARS
                   CR COUNT TYPE ."  ? "
               THEN doLIT .OK XOR
               IF $1B EMIT THEN
               PRESET
          AGAIN ;
```

5.0 eForth Compiler

After wading through the text interpreter, the Forth compiler will be an easy piece of cake, because the compiler uses almost all the modules used by the text interpreter. What the compile does, over and above the text interpreter, is to build various structures required by the new words we want to add to the existing system. Here is a list of these structures:

- **Name headers**
- **Colon definitions**
- **Constants,**
- **Variables**
- **User variables**
- **Integer literals**
- **String literals**   literals
- **Address literals**
- **Control structures**

A special concept of immediate words is difficult to grasp at first. It is required in the compiler because of the needs in building different data and control structures in a colon definition. To understand the Forth compiler fully, you have to be able to differential and relate the actions during compile time and actions taken during executing time. Once these concepts are clear, the whole Forth system will become transparent.

This set stage for enlightenment to strike.

5.1 Interpreter and Compiler

The Forth compiler is the twin brother of the Forth text interpreter. They share many common properties and use lots of common code. In eForth, the implementation of the compiler clearly reflects this special duality. Two interesting words [and] causes the text interpreter to switch back and forth between the compiler mode and interpreter mode of operation.

Since 'EVAL @EXECUTE is used in EVAL to process a word parsed out of a line of text, the contents in 'EVAL determines the behavior of the text interpreter. If $INTERPRET is stored in 'EVAL, as [does, the words are executed or interpreted.

If we invoked] to store $COMPILE into 'EVAL, the word will not be executed, but added to the top of the code dictionary. This is exactly the behavior desired by the colon definition compiler in building a list of words in the code field of a new colon definition on the top of the code dictionary.

$COMPILE normally adds a word to the code dictionary. However, there are two exceptions it must handle. If the word parsed out of the input stream does not exist in the dictionary, the string will be converted to a number.

If the string can be converted to an integer, the integer is then compiled into the code dictionary as an integer literal. The integer number is compiled into the code dictionary following the word doLIT. The other exception is that a word found in the dictionary could be an immediate word, which must be executed immediately, not compiled to the code dictionary. Immediate words are used to compile special structures in colon definitions.

```
: [  ( -- )
        [ '    $INTERPRET ] LITERAL
        'EVAL !                 ( vector EVAL to $INTERPRET )
        ; IMMEDIATE    ( enter into text interpreter mode )

: ]  ( -- )
        [ ' $COMPILE ] LITERAL
        'EVAL !                 ( vector EVAL to $COMPILE )
;
```

5.2 Primitive Compiler Words

Here is a group of words which support the compiler to build new words in the code dictionary.

' **(tick)** searches the next word in the input stream for a word in the dictionary. It returns the execution address of the word if successful. Otherwise, it displays an error message.

ALLOT allocates n bytes of memory on the top of the code dictionary. Once allocated, the compiler will not touch the memory locations.

, **(comma)** adds the execution address of a word on the top of the data stack to the code dictionary, and thus compiles a word to the growing word list of the word currently under construction.

COMPILE is used in a colon definition. It causes the next word after COMPILE to be added to the top of the code dictionary. It therefore forces the compilation of a word at the run time.

[COMPILE] acts similarly, except that it compiles the next word immediately. It causes the following word to be compiled, even if the following word is an immediate word which would otherwise be executed.

LITERAL compiles an integer literal to the current colon definition under construction. The integer literal is taken from the data stack, and is preceded by the word doLIT. When this colon definition is executed, doLIT will extract the integer from the word list and push it back on the data stack. LITERAL compiles an address literal if the compiled integer happens to be an execution address of a word. The address will be pushed on the data stack at the run time by doLIT.

$,"compiles a string literal. The string is taken from the input stream and is terminated by the double quote character. $," only copies the counted string to the code dictionary. A word which makes use of the counted string at the run time must be compiled before the string. It is used by ." and $".

RECURSE is an interesting word which allows eForth to compile recursive definitions. In a recursive definition, the execution address of the word under construction is compiled into its own word list. This is not allowed normally because the name field of the current word under construction is not yet linked to the current vocabulary and it cannot be referenced inside its own colon definition.

RECURSE stores the address of the name field of the current word into CURRENT, thus enable it to be referenced inside its own definition. Recursive words are not used in everyday programming. RECURSE is defined here in eForth merely as a teaser to wet your appetite. It is not used in eForth.

```
: '          ( -- xt ) TOKEN NAME? IF EXIT THEN THROW ;

: ALLOT      ( n -- )  CP +! ;

: ,          ( w -- )  HERE DUP CELL+ CP ! ! ; \ ???ALIGNED

: [COMPILE]  ( -- ; <string> ) ' , ; IMMEDIATE

: COMPILE    ( -- )    R> DUP @ , CELL+ >R ;

: LITERAL    ( w -- ) COMPILE doLIT , ; IMMEDIATE

: $,"        ( -- )    34 WORD COUNT ALIGNED CP ! ;

: RECURSE    ( -- )    LAST @ NAME> , ; IMMEDIATE
```

5.3 Structures

A set of immediate words are defined in eForth to help building control structures in colon definitions. The control structures used in eForth are the following:

Conditional branch	**IF** ...			**THEN**
	IF ...	**ELSE** ...		**THEN**
Finite loop	**FOR** ...			**NEXT**
	FOR ...	**AFT** ...	**THEN** ...	**NEXT**
Infinite loop	**BEGIN** ... **AGAIN**			
Indefinite loop	**BEGIN** ... **UNTIL**			
	BEGIN ... **WHILE** ...			**REPEAT**

This set of words is more powerful than the ones in the figForth model because they permit multiple exits from a loop. Many examples are provide in the source code of eForth like **NUMBER?**, parse, find and **>NAME**.

A control structure contains one or more address literals, which causes execution to branch out of the normal sequence. The control structure words are immediate words which compile the address literals and resolve the branch address.

One should note that BEGIN and THEN do not compile any code. They executes during compilation to set up and to resolve the branch addresses in the address literals. IF, ELSE, WHILE, UNTIL, and AGAIN do compile address literals with branching words. Here are many excellent examples on the usage of COMPILE and [COMPILE], and they are worthy of careful study.

Character strings are very important devices for the program to communicate with the user. Error messages, appropriate warnings and suggestions must be displayed to help the use to use the system in a friendly way. Character strings are compiled in the colon definitions as string literals.

Each string literal consists of a string word which will use the compiled string to do things, and a counted string. The first byte in a counted string is the length of the string. Thus, a string may have 0 to 255 characters in it. A string is always null-filled to the cell boundary.

ABORT" compiles an error message. This error message is display when the top item on the stack is non-zero. The rest of the words in the definition is skipped and eForth re-enters the interpreter loop. This is the universal response to an error condition. More sophisticated programmer can use the CATCH-THROW mechanism to customize the responses to special error conditions.

." compiles a character string which will be printed which the word containing it is executed in the runtime. This is the best way to present messages to the user.

$" compiles a character string. When it is executed, only the address of the string is left on the data stack. The programmer will use this address to access the string and individual characters in the string as a string array.

```
: <MARK      ( -- a )    HERE ;
: <RESOLVE   ( a -- )      , ;
: >MARK      ( -- A )    HERE 0 , ;
: >RESOLVE   ( A -- )    <MARK SWAP ! ;
```

```
: FOR        ( -- a )    COMPILE >R <MARK ; IMMEDIATE
: BEGIN      ( -- a )    <MARK ; IMMEDIATE
: NEXT       ( a -- )    COMPILE next <RESOLVE ; IMMEDIATE
: UNTIL      ( a -- )    COMPILE ?branch <RESOLVE ; IMMEDIATE
: AGAIN      ( a -- )    COMPILE  branch <RESOLVE ; IMMEDIATE
: IF         ( -- A )    COMPILE ?branch >MARK ; IMMEDIATE
: AHEAD      ( -- A )    COMPILE branch >MARK ; IMMEDIATE


: REPEAT     ( A a -- )   [COMPILE] AGAIN >RESOLVE ; IMMEDIATE
: THEN       ( A -- )        >RESOLVE ; IMMEDIATE
: AFT        ( a -- a A ) DROP [COMPILE] AHEAD [COMPILE] BEGIN
                         SWAP  ;  IMMEDIATE


: ELSE       ( A -- A )   [COMPILE] AHEAD SWAP [COMPILE] THEN ;
                         IMMEDIATE


: WHEN       ( a A -- a A a )   [COMPILE] IF OVER ; IMMEDIATE
: WHILE      ( a -- A a )       [COMPILE] IF SWAP ; IMMEDIATE


: ABORT"     ( -- ; <string> )   COMPILE abort" $," ; IMMEDIATE


: $"         ( -- ; <string> )   COMPILE $"| $," ; IMMEDIATE
: ."         ( -- ; <string> )   COMPILE ."| $," ; IMMEDIATE
```

5.4 Compiler

We had discussed how the compiler compiles words and structures into the code field of a colon definition in the code dictionary. To build a new definition, we have to build its header in the name dictionary also. A header has a word pointer field, a link field, and a name field. Here are the tools to build these fields.

?UNIQUE is used to display a warning message to show that the name of a new word is a duplicate to a word already existing in the dictionary. eForth does not mind your reusing the same name for different words. However, giving many words the same name is a potential cause of problems in maintaining software projects. It is to be avoided if possible and ?UNIQUE reminds you of it.

$,n builds a new entry in the name dictionary using the name already moved to the bottom of the name dictionary by PACK$. It pads the word field with the address of the top of code dictionary where the new code is to be built and link the link field to the current vocabulary. A new word can now be built in the code dictionary.

$COMPILE builds the body of a new colon definition. A complete colon definition also requires a header in the name dictionary, and its code field must start with a CALL doLIST instruction. These extra works are performed by :. Colon definitions are the most prevailing type of words in eForth. In addition, eForth has a few other defining words which create other types of new definitions in the dictionary.

OVERT links a new definition to the current vocabulary and thus makes it available for dictionary searches.

; terminates a colon definition. It compiles an EXIT to the end of the word list, links this new word to the current vocabulary, and then reactivates the interpreter.

] turns the interpreter to a compiler.

: creates a new header and start a new colon word. It takes the following string in the input stream to be the name of the new colon definition, by building a new header with this name in the name dictionary. It then compiles a CALL doLIST instruction at the beginning of the code field in the code dictionary. Now, the code dictionary is ready to accept a word list.] is now invoked to turn the text interpreter into a compiler, which will compile the following words in the input stream to a word list in the code dictionary.

The new colon definition is terminated by ;, which compiles an EXIT to terminate the word list, and executes [to turn the compiler back to text interpreter.

call, compiles the CALL doLIST instruction as the first thing in the code field of a colon definition.

IMMEDIATE sets the immediate lexicon bit in the name field of the new definition just compiled. When the compiler encounters a word with this bit set, it will not compile this word into the word list under construction, but execute the word immediately. This bit allows structure words to build special structures in the colon definitions, and to process special conditions when the compiler is running.

```
: ?UNIQUE  ( a -- a )
    DUP NAME? IF ." reDef " OVER COUNT TYPE THEN DROP ;


: $,n      ( a -- )
   DUP C@
   IF ?UNIQUE
     ( na) DUP LAST ! \ for OVERT
     ( na) HERE ALIGNED SWAP
     ( cp na) CELL-
     ( cp la) CURRENT @ @
     ( cp la na') OVER !
     ( cp la) CELL- DUP NP ! ( ptr) ! EXIT
   THEN $" name" THROW ;

.( FORTH Compiler )

: $COMPILE  ( a -- )
   NAME? ?DUP
   IF @ $80 AND
     IF EXECUTE ELSE , THEN EXIT
   THEN 'NUMBER @EXECUTE
   IF [COMPILE] LITERAL EXIT
   THEN THROW ;

: OVERT     ( -- ) LAST @ CURRENT @  ! ;

: ;         ( -- )
     COMPILE EXIT [COMPILE] [ OVERT ; IMMEDIATE

: ]         ( -- ) doLIT $COMPILE 'EVAL ! ;

: call,     ( xt -- )     \ DTC 8086 relative call
   $E890 , HERE CELL+ - , ;

: :         ( -- ; <string> ) TOKEN $,n doLIT doLIST  call, ] ;

: IMMEDIATE ( -- ) $80 LAST @ @ OR LAST @ ! ;
```

5.5 Defining Words

Defining words are molds which can be used to define many words
which share the same run time execution behavior. In eForth, we
have

    : , USER, CREATE, and VARIABLE.

USER creates a new user variable. The user variable contains an user
area offset, which is added to the beginning address of the user area
and to return the address of the user variable in the user area.
CREATE creates a new array without allocating memory. Memory is
allocated using ALLOT. VARIABLE creates a new variable, initialized
to 0.

eForth does not use CONSTANT, because an integer literal is more
economical than a constant. One can always use a variable for a
constant.

```
: USER ( n -- ; <string> )
        TOKEN $,n OVERT
        doLIT doLIST COMPILE doUSER , ;

: CREATE ( -- ; <string> )
        TOKEN $,n OVERT
        doLIT doLIST COMPILE doVAR ;

: VARIABLE ( -- ; <string> ) CREATE 0 , ;
```

6.0 Utilities

eForth is a very small system and only a very small set of tools are
provided in the system. Nevertheless, this set of tools is powerful
enough to help the user debug new words he adds to the system. They
are also very interesting programming examples on how to use the
words in eForth to build applications.

Generally, the tools present the information stored in different parts
of the memory in the appropriate format to let the use inspect the
results as he executes words in the eForth system and words he
defined himself.   The tools include memory dump, stack dump,
dictionary dump, and a colon definition decompiler.

6.1 Memory Dump

DUMP dumps u bytes starting at address b to the terminal. It dumps 16 bytes to a line. A line begins with the address of the first byte, followed by 16 bytes shown in hex, 3 columns per bytes. At the end of a line are the 16 bytes shown in characters. The character display is generated by _TYPE, which substitutes non-printable characters by underscores. Typing a key on the keyboard halts the display. Another CR terminates the display. Any other key resumes the display.

dm+ displays u bytes from b1 in one line. It leaves the address b1+u on the stack for the next dm+ command to use.

_TYPE is similar to **TYPE**. It displays u characters starting from b. Non-printable characters are replaced by underscores.

```
: _TYPE ( b u -- )
        FOR AFT DUP C@ >CHAR EMIT 1 + THEN NEXT DROP ;

: dm+   ( b u -- b )
        OVER 4 U.R SPACE FOR AFT DUP C@ 3 U.R 1 + THEN NEXT ;

: DUMP ( b u -- )
        BASE @ >R HEX   16 /
        FOR CR 16 2DUP dm+ ROT ROT 2 SPACES _
        TYPE NUF? NOT WHILE
        NEXT ELSE R> DROP THEN DROP  R> BASE ! ;
```

6.2 Stack Tools

Data stack is the working place of the Forth computer. It is where words receive their parameters and also where they left their results. In debugging a newly defined word which uses stack items, and which leaves items on the stack, the best was to check its function is to inspect the data stack.

The number output words may be used for this purpose, but they are destructive. You print out the number from the stack and it is gone. To inspect the data stack non-destructively, a special utility word .S is provided in most Forth systems. It is also implemented in eForth.

.S dumps the contents of the data stack on the screen in the free format. The bottom of the stack is aligned to the left margin. The top item is shown towards the left and followed by the characters '<sp'. .S does not change the data stack so it can be used to inspect the data stack non-destructively at any time.

One important discipline in learning Forth is to learn how to use the data stack effectively.   All words must consume their input parameters on the stack and leave only their intended results on the stack.

Sloppy usage of the data stack is often the cause of bugs which are very difficult to detect later as unexpected items left on the stack could result in unpredictable behavior. .S should be used liberally during Forth programming and debugging to ensure that the correct data are left on the data stack.

.S is useful in checking the stack interactively during the programming and debugging. It is not appropriate for checking the data stack at the run time. For run time stack checking, eForth provides !CSP and ?CSP. They are not used in the eForth system itself but are very useful for the user in developing serious applications.

To do run time stack checking, at some point the program should execute !CSP to mark the depth of the data stack at that point. Later, the program would execute ?CSP to see if the stack depth was changed.

Normally, the stack depth should be the same at these two points. If the stack depth is changed, ?CSP would abort the execution.
One application of stack checking is to ensure compiler security. Normally, compiling a colon definition does not change the depth of the data stack, if all the structure building immediate words in a colon definition are properly paired.

If they are not paired, like **IF** without a **THEN**, **FOR** without a **NEXT**, **BEGIN** without an **AGAIN** or **REPEAT**, etc., the data stack will not be balanced and ?CSP is very useful in catching these compilation errors. This stack check is a very simple but powerful tool to check the compiler.

!CSP and **CSP** are the words to monitor the stack depth.

!CSP stores the current data stack pointer into tan user variable **CSP**. The stack pointer saved will be used by ?CSP for error checking.

?CSP compares the current stack pointer with that saved in **CSP**. If they are different, abort and display the error message 'stack depth'.

```
: .S     ( -- )   CR DEPTH FOR AFT R@ PICK . THEN NEXT ." <sp" ;

: .BASE ( -- )   BASE @ DECIMAL DUP . BASE ! ;

: .FREE ( -- )   CP 2@ - U. ;

: !CSP   ( -- )   SP@ CSP ! ;

: ?CSP   ( -- )   SP@ CSP @ XOR ABORT" stack depth" ;
```

6.3 Dictionary Dump

The Forth dictionary contains all the words defined in the system, ready for execution and compilation. **WORDS** allows you to examine the dictionary and to look for the correct names of words in case you are not sure of their spellings.

WORDS follows the vocabulary thread in the user variable **CONTEXT** and displays the names of each entry in the name dictionary. The vocabulary thread can be traced easily because the link field in the header of a word points to the name field of the previous word. The link field of the next word is one cell below its name field.

WORDS displays all the names in the context vocabulary. The order of words is reversed from the compiled order. The last defined words is shown first.

.ID displays the name of a word, given the word's name field address. It also replaces non-printable characters in a name by under-scores. Since the name fields are linked into a list in the name dictionary, it is fairly easy to locate a word by searching its name in the name dictionary.

However, finding the name of a word from the execution address of the word is more difficult, because the execution addresses of words are not organized in any systematic way.

It is necessary to find the name of a word from its execution address, if we wanted to decompile the contents of a word list in the code dictionary. This reversed search is accomplished by the word >NAME.

>NAME finds the name field address of a word from the execution address of the word. If the word does not exist in the **CURRENT** vocabulary, it returns a false flag. It is the mirror image of the word **NAME>**, which returns the execution address of a word from its name address. Since the execution address of a word is stored in the word field, two cells below the name, **NAME>** is trivial.

>NAME is more complicated because the entire name dictionary must be searched to locate the word. **>NAME** only searches the **CURRENT** vocabulary.

Bill Muench and I spent much of our spare time in July, 1991 to build and polish the eForth Model and the first implementation on 8086/MS-DOS. One evening he called me and told me about this smallest and greatest Forth decompiler, only three lines of source code. I was very skeptical because I knew how to build a Forth decompiler.

If a Forth colon definition contains only a simple list of execution addresses, it is a trivial task to decompile it. However, there are many different data and control structures in a colon definition. To deal with all these structures, it is logically impossible to have a three line decompiler.

I told Bill that I had to see it to believe. The next time we met, he read the source code in assembly and I entered it into the eForth model. The decompiler had 24 words and worked the first time after we reassembled the source code.

SEE searches the dictionary for the next word in the input stream and returns its code field address. Then it scans the list of execution addresses (words) in the colon definition. If the word fetched out of the list matches the execution address of a word in the name dictionary, the name will be displayed by the command '.ID'. If the word does not match any execution address in the name dictionary, it must be part of a structure and it is displayed by 'U.'.

This way, the decompiler ignores all the data structures and control structures in the colon definition, and only displays valid words in the word list.

```
: >NAME ( xt -- na | F )
        CURRENT
        BEGIN CELL+ @ ?DUP WHILE 2DUP
        BEGIN @ DUP WHILE 2DUP NAME> XOR
        WHILE CELL-
        REPEAT       THEN SWAP DROP ?DUP
        UNTIL SWAP DROP SWAP DROP EXIT THEN DROP 0 ;

: .ID ( a -- )
        ?DUP IF COUNT $01F AND _TYPE EXIT THEN ." {noName}" ;

: SEE ( -- ; <string> )
        ' CR CELL+
        BEGIN CELL+ DUP @ DUP IF >NAME THEN ?DUP
        IF SPACE .ID ELSE DUP @ U. THEN NUF?
        UNTIL DROP ;

: WORDS ( -- )
        CR  CONTEXT @
        BEGIN @ ?DUP
        WHILE DUP SPACE .ID CELL-  NUF?
        UNTIL DROP THEN ;
```

6.4 Startup

Since we expect eForth to evolve as experience is accumulated with usage, and as it has to track the **ANS Forth Standard** under development, version control becomes an important issue. To assure compatibility at different stages of development, the user can always inquire the version number of the eForth he is running. With the version number, corrective actions can be taken to put an overlay on the system to force it to be compatible with another eForth of a different version.

VER returns the version number of this eForth system. The version number contains two bytes: the most significant byte is the major revision number, and the least significant byte is the minor release number.

'hi' is he default start-up routine in eForth. It initializes the serial I/O device and then displays a sign-on message. This is where the user can customize his application. From here on he can initialize the system to start his customized application.

Because all the system variables in eForth are implemented as user variables and the name dictionary is separated from the code dictionary, the eForth dictionary is eminently ROMable and most suitable for embedded applications. To be useful as a generic model for many different processors and applications, a flexible mechanism is designed to help booting eForth up in different environments.

Before falling into the QUIT loop, the COLD routine executes a boot routine whose code address is stored in 'BOOT. This code address can

be vectored to an application routine which defines the proper
behavior of the system.

After the computer is turned on, it executes some native machine
code to set up the CPU hardware so that it emulates a virtual Forth
computer. Then it jumps to **COLD** to initialize the eForth system. It
finally jumps to **QUIT** which is the operating system in eForth. **COLD**
and **QUIT** are the topmost layers of an eForth system.

'BOOT is an variable vectored to 'hi'.

COLD is a high level word executed upon power-up. Its most
important function is to initialize the user area and execute the boot-
up routine vectored through **'BOOT**, and then falls into the text
interpreter loop **QUIT**.

```
: VER ( -- u ) $101 ;

: hi ( -- )
        !IO BASE @ HEX \ initialize IO device & sign on
        CR ." eFORTH V" VER <# # # 46 HOLD # #> TYPE
        CR ;

: EMPTY ( -- )
        FORTH CONTEXT @ DUP CURRENT 2!   6 CP 3 MOVE OVERT ;

CREATE 'BOOT   ' hi , \ application vector

: COLD ( -- )
        BEGIN
        U0 UP 74 CMOVE
        PRESET   'BOOT @EXECUTE
          FORTH CONTEXT @ DUP CURRENT 2! OVERT
```

```
QUIT
AGAIN ;
```

6.5 ColdBoot from DOS

DOS starts executing the object code at 100H. The eForth Model is configured for a DOS machine. It can be modified to jump to any memory location from where the CPU boots up. What we have to do here is to set up the 8086 CPU so that it will emulate the virtual Forth computer as we discussed before.

All the pertinent registers have to be initialized properly. Since eForth is very small and fits comfortably in a single 64 Kbyte code segment, we will use only one segment for code, data, as well as the two stacks. Therefore, both the DS and SS segment registers are initialized to be the same as the CS register.

Then, the data stack pointer SP and the return stack pointer RP (BP in 8086) are initialized. To prevent the eForth from being forced back into DOS accidentally, the Control-C interrupt is made benign by vectoring it to a simple IRET instruction.

Now we are ready to start the Forth computer. Simply jumping to COLD will do it. COLD is coded as a colon word, containing a list of words.

This word list does more initialization in high level, including initializing the user area, and setting up the terminal input buffer. At the end, COLD executes QUIT, the text interpreter, which contains an infinite loop to receive commands from a user and executes them repeatedly.

The user area contains vital information for Forth to perform its functions. It contains important pointers specifying memory areas for various activities, such as the data stack, the return stack, the terminal input buffer, where the code dictionary and the name dictionary end, and the execution addresses of many vectored words like KEY, EMIT, ECHO, EXPECT, NUMBER, etc.

The user area must be located in the RAM memory, because the information contained in it are continuously updated when eForth is running. The default values are stored in the code segment starting at UZERO and covering an area of 74 bytes.

This area is copied to the user area in RAM before starting the eForth computer. The sequence of data in UZERO must match exactly the sequence of user variables.

```
;; Main entry points and COLD start data
MAIN    SEGMENT
ASSUME  CS:MAIN,DS:MAIN,ES:MAIN,SS:MAIN
ORG     COLDD                       ;beginning of cold boot
ORIG:   MOV     AX,CS
        MOV     DS,AX               ;DS is same as CS
        CLI                         ;disable interrupts, old 808x CPU bug
        MOV     SS,AX               ;SS is same as CS
        MOV     SP,SPP              ;initialize SP
        STI                         ;enable interrupts
        MOV     BP,RPP              ;initialize RP
        MOV     AL,023H             ;interrupt 23H
        MOV     DX,OFFSET CTRLC
        MOV     AH,025H             ;MS-DOS set interrupt vector
        INT     021H
        CLD                         ;direction flag, increment
        JMP     COLD                ;to high level cold start
CTRLC:  IRET                        ;control C interrupt routine
```

```
; COLD start moves the following to USER variables.
; MUST BE IN SAME ORDER AS USER VARIABLES.
$ALIGN                   ;align to cell boundary
UZERO: DW    4 DUP (0)   ;reserved
       DW    SPP         ;SP0
       DW    RPP         ;RP0
       DW    QRX         ;'?KEY
       DW    TXSTO       ;'EMIT
       DW    ACCEP       ;'EXPECT
       DW    KTAP        ;'TAP
       DW    TXSTO       ;'ECHO
       DW    DOTOK       ;'PROMPT
       DW    BASEE       ;BASE
       DW    0           ;tmp
       DW    0           ;SPAN
       DW    0           ;>IN
       DW    0           ;#TIB
       DW    TIBB        ;TIB
       DW    0           ;CSP
       DW    INTER       ;'EVAL
       DW    NUMBQ       ;'NUMBER
       DW    0           ;HLD
       DW    0           ;HANDLER
       DW    0           ;CONTEXT pointer
       DW    VOCSS DUP (0)    ;vocabulary stack
       DW    0           ;CURRENT pointer
       DW    0           ;vocabulary link pointer
       DW    CTOP        ;CP
       DW    NTOP        ;NP
       DW    LASTN       ;LAST
ULAST:
```

7.0 Some Final Thoughts

Congratulations, if you reach this point the first time. As you can see, we have traversed a complete Forth system from the beginning to the end, and it is not as difficult as you might have thought before you began. But, think again what we have accomplished.

It is a complete operating system with an integrated interpreter and an integrated compiler all together. If you look in the memory, the whole system is less than 7 Kbytes. What else can you do with 7 Kbytes these days?

Forth is like Zen. It is simple, it is accessible, and it can be understood in its entirety without devoting your whole life to it.

Is this the end? Not really. There are many topics important in Forth but we had chose to ignore in this simple model. They include multitasking, virtual memory, interrupt control, programming style, source code management, and yes, metacompilation. However, these topics can be considered advanced applications of Forth. Once the fundamental principles in Forth are understood, these topics can be subject for further investigations at your leisure.

Forth is not an end to itself. It is only a tool, as useful as the user intends it to be. The most important thing is how the user can use it to solve his problems and build useful applications. What eForth gives you is the understanding of this tool. It is up to you to make use of it.

End of the original document
V5 2016_09_07 v4_2018_10_19

8   Extracted eForth Code

The following pages are additional material generated by Juergen Pintaske, ExMark.
It is the same code as in the pages before,
but with the text removed and the code blocks numbered for people who want to look
at the eForth code and the structure more closely.

The same information can be found in the Forth-eV Wiki page
https://wiki.forth-ev.de/doku.php/en:projects:430eforth:start
for download and print.
There you can find as well the code as one big page for print.
Size about 60x70 cm; the same as seen on the first page – but more readable ...

eForth Overview by C. H. Ting

```
Here just code. The complete file can be found at www.exemark.com under Forth

\ The following registers are required
\ for a virtual Forth computer:
\  Forth Register    8086 Register    Function
\  IP                SI               Interpreter Pointer
\  SP                SP               Data Stack Pointer
\  RP                RP               Return Stack Pointer
\  WP                AX               Word or Work Pointer
\  UP                (in memory )     User Area Pointer

Variable IP    \ Interpreter  Pointer
Variable SP    \ Data Stack   Pointer
Variable RP    \ Return Stack Pointer
Variable WP    \ Word or Work Pointer
Variable UP    \ User Area    Pointer

\ $NEXT      MACRO                        \ ------------------------------1
\            LODSW                        \ load next word into WP (AX)
\            JMP      AX                  \ jump directly to the word thru WP
\            ENDM                         \ IP (SI) now points to the next word
\ doLIST     ( a -- )                     \ Run address list in a colon word.   \ 2
\            XCHG     BP,SP               \ exchange pointers
\            PUSH     SI                  \ push return stack
\            XCHG     BP,SP               \ restore the pointers
\            POP      SI                  \ new list address
\            $NEXT
\ CODE EXIT                              \ Terminate a colon definition.   \ 3
\            XCHG     BP,SP               \ exchange pointers
\            POP      SI                  \ pop return stack
\            XCHG     BP,SP               \ restore the pointers
\            $NEXT

\ 1.2   Memory Map - Memory used
\       in eForth is separated into the following areas:

\ Cold boot         100H-17FH        Cold start and variable initial values
\ Code dictionary   180H-1344H       Code dictionary growing upward
\ Free space        1346H-33E4H      Shared by code/name dictionaries
\ Name/word         33E6H-3BFFH      Name dictionary growing downward
\ Data stack        3C00H-3E7FH      Growing downward
\ TIB               3E80H-           Growing upward
\ Return stack      -3F7FH               Growing downward
\ User variables    3F80H-3FFFH

\ ;; Memory allocation
\ ;; 0//code>--//--<name//up>--<sp//tib>--rp//em
```

BP R

```
\ EM      EQU   04000H            ;top of memory
\ COLDD   EQU   00100H            ;cold start vector
\ US      EQU   64*CELLL          ;user area size in cells
\ RTS     EQU   64*CELLL          ;return stack/TIB size
\ RPP     EQU   EM-8*CELLL        ;start of return stack (RP0)
\ TIBB    EQU   RPP-RTS           ;terminal input buffer (TIB)
\ SPP     EQU   TIBB-8*CELLL      ;start of data stack (SP0)
\ UPP     EQU   EM-256*CELLL      ;start of user area (UP0)
\ NAMEE   EQU   UPP-8*CELLL       ;name dictionary
\ CODEE   EQU   COLDD+US          ;code dictionary

\ 2.0   eForth Kernel
\ System interface:    BYE,    ?rx,     tx!,     !io
\ Inner interpreters:  doLIT,  doLIST,  next,    ?branch,  branch,  EXECUTE,  EXIT
\ Memory access:       !,      @,       C!,      C@
\ Return stack:        RP@,    RP!,     R>,      R@,       R>
\ Data stack:          SP@,    SP!,     DROP,    DUP,      SWAP,    OVER
\ Logic:               0<,     AND,     OR,      XOR
\ Arithmetic:          UM+

\ 2.1   System Interface
\   CODE BYE ( -- , exit Forth )            \ ------------------------------ 4
\              INT    020H                  \ return to DOS
\
\ CODE   ?RX   ( -- c T | F )               \ Return input character and true,  \ --5
\                                           \ or a false if no input.
\               $CODE   3,'?RX',QRX
\               XOR     BX,BX               \ BX=0 setup for false flag
\               MOV     DL,0FFH             \ input command
\               MOV     AH,6                \ MS-DOS Direct Console I/O
\               INT     021H
\               JZ      QRX3                \ ?key ready
\               OR      AL,AL               \ AL=0 if extended char
\               JNZ     QRX1                \ ?extended character code
\               INT     021H
\               MOV     BH,AL               \ extended code in msb
\               JMP     QRX2
\ QRX1:         MOV     BL,AL
\ QRX2:         PUSH    BX                  \ save character
\               MOV     BX,-1               \ true flag
\ QRX3:         PUSH    BX
\               $NEXT
\
\ CODE   TX!   ( c -- )                     \ Send character c to output device. \ --- 6
\               POP     DX                  \ char in DL
\               CMP     DL,0FFH             \ 0FFH is interpreted as input
\               JNZ     TX1                 \ do NOT allow input
\               MOV     DL,32               \ change to blank
\ TX1:          MOV     AH,6                \ MS-DOS Direct Console I/O
\               INT     021H               \ display character
\               $NEXT
\
\ CODE   !IO   ( -- )                       \ Initialize the serial I/O devices.  \ --7
\               $NEXT

\ 2.2   Inner Interpreter
\ $NEXT  MACRO                              \ ------------------------------------ 8
\        LODSW                              \ load next word into WP (AX)
\        JMP     AX                         \ jump directly to the word thru WP
\        ENDM                               \ IP (SI) now points to the next word
\
\ doLIST ( a -- )                           \ Run address list in a colon word.   \ 9
\        XCHG    BP,SP                       \ exchange pointers
\        PUSH    SI                          \ push return stack
\        XCHG    BP,SP                       \ restore the pointers
\        POP     SI                          \ new list address
\        $NEXT
\
\ CODE   EXIT                               \ Terminate a colon definition.    \ -- 10
\        XCHG    BP,SP                       \ exchange pointers
\        POP     SI                          \ pop return stack
\        XCHG    BP,SP                       \ restore the pointers
\        $NEXT
\
\ CODE   EXECUTE   ( ca -- )                \ Execute the word at ca.          \ -- 11
\        POP     BX
\        JMP     BX                          \ jump to the code address
\
\ CODE   doLIT   ( -- w )                   \ Push inline literal on data stack. \ 12
\        LODSW                               \ get the literal compiled in-line
\        PUSH    AX                          \ push literal on the stack
\        $NEXT                               \ execute next word after literal
```

```
\ 2.3  Loops and Branches
\ CODE  next ( -- )                   \ Decrement index and exit loop      \ - 13
\                                     \ if index is less than 0.
\             SUB    WORD PTR [BP],1  \ decrement the index
\             JC     NEXT1            \ ?decrement below 0
\             MOV    SI,0[SI]         \ no, continue loop
\             $NEXT
\ NEXT1:      ADD    BP,2             \ yes, pop the index
\             ADD    SI,2             \ exit loop
\             $NEXT
\
\ CODE  ?branch  ( f -- )            \ Branch if flag is zero.             \---14
\             POP    BX               \ pop flag
\             OR     BX,BX            \ ?flag=0
\             JZ     BRAN1            \ yes, so branch
\             ADD    SI,2             \ point IP to next cell
\             $NEXT
\ BRAN1:      MOV    SI,0[SI]         \ IP:=(IP), jump to new address
\             $NEXT
\
\ CODE  branch  ( -- )               \ Branch to an inline address.        \ --15
\             MOV    SI,0[SI]         \ jump to new address unconditionally
\             $NEXT

\ 2.4  Memory Access
\ CODE  !        ( w a -- )          \ Pop the data stack to memory.       \ --16
\             POP    BX               \ get address from tos
\             POP    0[BX]            \ store data to that adddress
\             $NEXT
\
\ CODE  @        ( a -- w )          \ Push memory location to data stack. \ 17
\             POP    BX               \ get address
\             PUSH   0[BX]            \ fetch data
\             $NEXT
\
\ CODE  C!    ( c b -- )             \ Pop data stack to byte memory.      \ --18
\             POP    BX               \ get address
\             POP    AX               \ get data in a cell
\             MOV    0[BX],AL         \ store one byte
\             $NEXT
\
\ CODE  C@   ( b -- c )              \ Push byte memory content on data stack. \ 19
\             POP    BX               \ get address
\             XOR    AX,AX            \ AX=0 zero the hi byte
\             MOV    AL,0[BX]         \ get low byte
\             PUSH   AX               \ push on stack
\             $NEXT

\ 2.5  Return Stack
\ CODE  RP@      ( -- a )            \ Push current RP to data stack.      \ -- 20
\             PUSH   BP               \ copy address to return stack
\             $NEXT                   \ pointer register BP
\
\ CODE  RP!      ( a -- )            \ Set the return stack pointer.       \ ---- 21
\             POP    BP               \ copy (BP) to tos
\             $NEXT
\
\ CODE  R>       ( -- w )            \ Pop return stack to data stack.     \ -- 22
\             PUSH   0[BP]            \ copy w to data stack
\             ADD    BP,2             \ adjust RP for popping
\             $NEXT
\
\ CODE  R@       ( -- w )            \ Copy top of return stack to data stack. \ 23
\             PUSH   0[BP]            \ copy w to data stack
\             $NEXT
\
\ CODE  >R       ( w -- )            \ Push data stack to return stack.    \ -- 24
\             SUB    BP,2             \ adjust RP for pushing
\             POP    0[BP]            \ push w to return stack
\             $NEXT

\ 2.6  Data Stack
\ CODE  DROP   ( w -- ) \ Discard top stack item.                         \ ----------- 25
\             ADD    SP,2             \ adjust SP to pop
\             $NEXT
\
\ CODE  DUP    ( w -- w w )  \ Duplicate the top stack item.              \ 26
\             MOV    BX,SP            \ use BX to index the stack
\             PUSH   0[BX]
\             $NEXT
\
\ CODE  SWAP   ( w1 w2 -- w2 w1 ) \ Exchange top two stack items.         \ 27
\             POP    BX               \ get w2
```

```
\          POP       AX              \ get w1
\          PUSH      BX              \ push w2
\          PUSH      AX              \ push w1
\          $NEXT
\ CODE   OVER      ( w1 w2 -- w1 w2 w1 ) \ Copy second stack item to top    \ 28
\          MOV       BX,SP                   \ use BX to index the stack
\          PUSH      2[BX]                 \ get w1 and push on stack
\          $NEXT
\ CODE   SP@       ( -- a )        \ Push the current data stack pointer.    \ 29
\          MOV       BX,SP               \ use BX to index the stack
\          PUSH      BX      \ push SP back
\          $NEXT
\ CODE   SP!       ( a -- )      \ Set the data stack pointer.               \ 30
\          POP       SP            \ safety
\          $NEXT
```

```
\ 2.7   Logical Words
\ CODE   0<        ( n -- f )      \ Return true if n is negative.            \ --- 31
\          POP       AX
\          CWD                    \ sign extend AX into DX
\          PUSH      DX      \ push 0 or -1
\          $NEXT
\ CODE   AND       ( w w -- w )    \ Bitwise AND.                             \ ---- 32
\          POP       BX
\          POP       AX
\          AND       BX,AX
\          PUSH      BX
\          $NEXT
\ CODE   OR        ( w w -- w )    \ Bitwise inclusive OR.                    \ 33
\          POP       BX
\          POP       AX
\          OR        BX,AX
\          PUSH      BX
\          $NEXT
\ CODE   XOR       ( w w -- w )    \ Bitwise exclusive OR.                    \ 34
\          POP       BX
\          POP       AX
\          XOR       BX,AX
\          PUSH      BX
\          $NEXT
```

```
\ 2.8   Primitive Arithmetic
\ CODE   UM+     ( w w -- w cy )     \            ---------------------------- 35
\                                   \ Add two numbers,
\                                   \ return the sum and carry flag.
\          XOR       CX,CX       \ CX=0 initial carry flag
\          POP       BX
\          POP       AX
\          ADD       AX,BX
\          RCL       CX,1        \ get carry
\          PUSH      AX            \ push sum
\          PUSH      CX            \ push carry
\          $NEXT
```

```
\ 3.0   High Level Forth Words
\ 3.1   Variables  and User Variables
\ : doVAR ( -- a ) R> ;  \ starting at 100 rather than continue              \ 101

\ VARIABLE UP ( -- a, Pointer to the user area.)                             \ ------ - 102

\ : doUSER       ( -- a, Run time routine for user variables.)               \ -- 103
\          R> @              \ retrieve user area offset
\          UP @ + ;                \ add to user area base addr

\ : doVOC  ( -- ) R> CONTEXT ! ;                          \ -------------------- 104
\ : FORTH  ( -- ) doVOC [ 0 , 0 ,                         \ -------------------- 105
\ : doUSER ( -- a ) R> @ UP @ + ;                         \ -------------------- 106

\ SP0      ( -- a, pointer to bottom of the data stack.)                     \ 107
\ RP0      ( -- a, pointer to bottom of the return stack.)                   \ 108
\ '?KEY    ( -- a, execution vector of ?KEY. \ Default to ?rx.)              \ 109
\ 'EMIT    ( -- a, execution vector of EMIT. \ Default to tx!)               \ 110

\ 'EXPECT  ( -- a, execution vector of EXPECT.  Default to 'accept'.)        \ 111

\ 'TAP     ( -- a, execution vector of TAP.  Defulat the kTAP.)              \ 112
```

```
\ 'ECHO     ( -- a, execution vector of ECHO.  Default to tx!.)          \ 113

\ 'PROMPT   ( -- a, execution vector of PROMPT.  Default to '.ok'.)       \ 115

\ BASE      ( -- a,.radix base for numeric I/O.  \ Default to 10.)        \ 116

\ tmp       ( -- a, a temporary storage location used in parse and find.) \ 117

\ SPAN      ( -- a, hold character count received by EXPECT.)             \ 118
\ >IN       ( -- a, hold the character pointer                            \ 119
\               while parsing input stream.)

\ #TIB      ( -- a, hold the current count and address                    \ 120
\               of the terminal input buffer.
\               Terminal Input Buffer used one cell after #TIB.)

\ CSP       ( -- a, hold the stack pointer for error checking.)           \ 121
\ 'EVAL     ( -- a, execution vector of EVAL. Default to EVAL.)           \ 122
\ 'NUMBER   ( -- a, address of number conversion.                        \ 123
\               Default to NUMBER?.)
\ HLD       ( -- a, hold a pointer in building a numeric output string.)  \ 124

\ HANDLER   ( -- a, hold the return stack pointer for error              \ 125
\               handling.)
\ CONTEXT   ( -- a, a area to specify vocabulary search order            \ 126
\               Default to FORTH.
\               Vocabulary stack, 8 cells follwing CONTEXT.)
\ CURRENT   ( -- a, point to the vocabulary to be extended.              \ 127
\               Default to FORTH.
\               Vocabulary link uses one cell after CURRENT.)
\ CP        ( -- a, point to the top of the code dictionary.)            \ 128
\ NP        ( -- a, point to the bottom of the name dictionary.)         \ 129
\ LAST      ( -- a, point to the last name in the name dictionary.)
\                                                                         \ 130
```

```
\ 3.2   Common Functions
\  ?DUP   ROT   2DROP   and  2DUP  \  are stack operators supplementing
\                                  \  the four classic stack operators
\  DUP    SWAP   OVER   and  DROP.

\ : ?DUP    ( w -- w w | 0 )        DUP IF DUP THEN ;                     \ 131
\ : ROT     ( w1 w2 w3 -- w2 w3 w1 ) >R SWAP R> SWAP ;                    \ 132
\ : 2DROP   ( w w -- )              DROP DROP ;                           \ 133
\ : 2DUP    ( w1 w2 -- w1 w2 w1 w2 ) OVER OVER ;                          \ 134
\ : +       ( w w -- w )            UM+ DROP ;                            \ 135
\ : NOT     ( w -- w )              -1 XOR ;                              \ 136
\ : NEGATE  ( n -- -n )             NOT 1 + ;                             \ 137
\ : DNEGATE ( d -- -d )             NOT >R NOT 1 UM+ R> + ;               \ 138
\ : D+      ( d d -- d )            >R SWAP >R UM+ R> R> + + ;            \ 139
\ : -       ( w w -- w )            NEGATE + ;                            \ 140
\ : ABS     ( n -- +n )             DUP 0< IF NEGATE THEN ;               \ 141
```

```
\ 3.3   Comparison
\ : =       ( w w -- t )     XOR IF 0 EXIT THEN -1 ;                            \ 142
\ : U<      ( u u -- t )     2DUP XOR 0< IF SWAP DROP 0< EXIT THEN - 0< ; \     \ 143
\ : <       ( n n -- t )     2DUP XOR 0< IF      DROP 0< EXIT THEN - 0< ; \     \ 144
\ : MAX     ( n n -- n )     2DUP    < IF SWAP THEN DROP ;                      \ 145
\ : MIN     ( n n -- n )     2DUP SWAP < IF SWAP THEN DROP ;                    \ 146
\ : WITHIN  ( u ul uh -- t ) OVER - >R - R> U< ;   \ ul <= u < uh              \ 147
```

```
\ 3.4   Divide
\ : UM/MOD  ( ud u -- ur uq )                                             \ 148
\   2DUP U<
\   IF NEGATE  15
\     FOR >R DUP UM+ >R >R DUP UM+ R> + DUP
\       R> R@ SWAP >R UM+ R> OR
\         IF >R DROP 1 + R> ELSE DROP THEN R>
\     NEXT DROP SWAP EXIT
\   THEN DROP 2DROP  -1 DUP ;

\ : M/MOD   ( d n -- r q ) \ floored division                            \ 149
\   DUP 0<  DUP >R
\   IF NEGATE >R DNEGATE R>
\   THEN >R DUP 0< IF R@ + THEN R> UM/MOD R>
\   IF SWAP NEGATE SWAP THEN ;

\ : /MOD    ( n n -- r q ) OVER 0< SWAP M/MOD ;                          \ 150
\ : MOD     ( n n -- r ) /MOD DROP ;                                     \ 151
\ : /       ( n n -- q ) /MOD SWAP DROP ;                                \ 152
```

```
\ 3.5  Multiply
\ : UM*     ( u u -- ud )                                                 \ 153
\   0 SWAP  ( u1 0 u2 )  15
```

```
\       FOR DUP UM+ >R >R DUP UM+ R> + R>
\         IF >R OVER UM+ R> + THEN
\       NEXT ROT DROP ;                                              \ 154
\   : *          ( n n -- n ) UM* DROP ;                             \ 155
\   : M*         ( n n -- d )
\       2DUP XOR 0< >R  ABS SWAP ABS UM*  R> IF DNEGATE THEN ;       \ 156
\   : */MOD      ( n n n -- r q ) >R M* R> M/MOD ;                   \ 157
\   : */         ( n n n -- q ) */MOD SWAP DROP ;

\ 3.6  Memory  Alignment                                            \ 158
\   : CELL-      ( a -- a )  -2 + ;                                  \ 159
\   : CELL+      ( a -- a )   2 + ;                                  \ 160
\   : CELLS      ( n -- n )   2 * ;                                  \ 161
\   : ALIGNED    ( b -- a )
\       DUP 0 2 UM/MOD DROP DUP
\       IF 2 SWAP - THEN + ;                                         \ 162
\   : BL         ( -- 32 ) 32 ;                                      \ 163
\   : >CHAR      ( c -- c )
\       $7F AND DUP 127 BL WITHIN IF DROP 95 THEN ;                  \ 164
\   : DEPTH      ( -- n ) SP@ SP0 @ SWAP - 2 / ;                     \ 165
\   : PICK       ( +n -- w ) 1 + CELLS SP@ + @ ;

\ 3.7  Memory  Access                                               \ 166
\   : +!         ( n a -- ) SWAP OVER @ + SWAP ! ;                   \ 167
\   : 2!         ( d a -- ) SWAP OVER ! CELL+ ! ;                    \ 168
\   : 2@         ( a -- d ) DUP CELL+ @ SWAP @ ;                     \ 169
\   : COUNT      ( b -- b +n ) DUP 1 + SWAP C@ ;                     \ 170
\   : HERE       ( -- a ) CP @ ;                                     \ 171
\   : PAD        ( -- a ) HERE 80 + ;                                \ 172
\   : TIB        ( -- a ) #TIB CELL+ @ ;                             \ 173
\   : @EXECUTE   ( a -- ) @ ?DUP IF EXECUTE THEN ;                   \ 174
\   : CMOVE      ( b b u -- )
\       FOR AFT >R DUP C@ R@ C! 1 + R> 1 + THEN NEXT 2DROP ;         \ 175
\   : FILL       ( b u c -- )
\       SWAP FOR SWAP AFT 2DUP C! 1 + THEN NEXT 2DROP ;              \ 176
\   : -TRAILING  ( b u -- b u )
\       FOR AFT BL OVER R@ + C@ <
\       IF R> 1 + EXIT THEN THEN
\       NEXT 0 ;                                                     \ 177
\   : PACK$      ( b u a -- a ) \ null fill
\       ALIGNED  DUP >R OVER
\       DUP 0 2 UM/MOD DROP
\       - OVER +  0 SWAP !  2DUP C!  1 + SWAP CMOVE  R> ;

\ 4.0  Text Interpreter
\       Accept text input from a terminal
\       Parse out commands from input text
\       Search dictionary
\       Execute commands
\       Translate numbers into binary
\       Display numbers in text form
\       Handle errors gracefully

\ 4.1  Numeric Output                                               \ 178
\   : DIGIT      ( u -- c )      9 OVER < 7 AND + 48 + ;
\   : EXTRACT    ( n base -- n c ) 0 SWAP UM/MOD SWAP DIGIT ;        \ 179
\   : <#         ( -- )          PAD HLD ! ;                         \ 180
\   : HOLD       ( c -- )        HLD @ 1 - DUP HLD ! C! ;            \ 181
\   : #          ( u -- u )      BASE @ EXTRACT HOLD ;               \ 182
\   : #S         ( u -- 0 )      BEGIN # DUP WHILE REPEAT ;          \ 183
\   : SIGN       ( n -- )        0< IF 45 HOLD THEN ;                \ 184
\   : #>         ( w -- b u )    DROP HLD @ PAD OVER - ;             \ 185
\   : str        ( n -- b u )    DUP >R ABS <# #S R> SIGN #> ;       \ 186
\   : HEX        ( -- )          16 BASE ! ;                         \ 187
\   : DECIMAL    ( -- )          10 BASE ! ;                         \ 188

\ 4.2  Number Output
\   : str        ( n -- b u )                                        \ 189
\       ( Convert a signed integer to a numeric string.)
\       DUP >R    ( save a copy for sign)
\       ABS       ( use absolute of n)
\       <# #S     ( convert all digits)
\       R> SIGN   ( add sign from n)
\       #> ;      ( return number string addr and length)
\   : HEX        ( -- )                                              \ 190
\       ( Use radix 16 as base for numeric conversions.)
\       16 BASE ! ;
\   : DECIMAL    ( -- )                                              \ 191
\       ( Use radix 10 as base for numeric conversions.)
\       10 BASE ! ;
\   : .R         ( n +n -- )  \ Display an integer in a field        \ 192
\                             of n columns, right justified.)
\       >R str    ( convert n to a number string)
```

111

```
\        R> OVER - SPACES ( print leading spaces)
\        TYPE ;    ( print number in +n column format)
\ : U.R        ( u +n -- )                                          \ 193
\             ( Display an unsigned integer in n column,
\               right justified.)
\        >R    ( save column number)
\        <# #S #> R> ( convert unsigned number)
\        OVER - SPACES ( print leading spaces)
\        TYPE ;    ( print number in +n columns)
\ : U.         ( u -- )                                             \ 194
\             ( Display an unsigned integer in free format.)
\        <# #S #> ( convert unsigned number)
\        SPACE    ( print one leading space)
\        TYPE ;    ( print number)
\ : .          ( w -- )                                             \ 195
\             ( Display an integer in free format,
\               preceeded by a space.)
\        BASE @ 10 XOR   ( if not in decimal mode)
\         IF U. EXIT THEN ( print unsigned number)
\        str SPACE TYPE ;( print signed number if decimal)
\ : ?          ( a -- )                                             \ 196
\             ( Display the contents in a memory cell.)
\        @ . ;    ( very simple but useful command)

\ 4.3  Numeric Input
\ : DIGIT?     ( c base -- u t )                                    \ 197
\        >R 48 - 9 OVER <
\        IF 7 - DUP 10 < OR THEN DUP R> U< ;
\ : NUMBER?    ( a -- n T | a F )                                   \ 198
\        BASE @ >R  0 OVER COUNT ( a 0 b n)
\        OVER C@ 36 =
\        IF HEX SWAP 1 + SWAP 1 - THEN ( a 0 b' n')
\        OVER C@ 45 = >R ( a 0 b n)
\        SWAP R@ - SWAP R@ + ( a 0 b" n") ?DUP
\        IF 1 - ( a 0 b n)
\          FOR DUP >R C@ BASE @ DIGIT?
\            WHILE SWAP BASE @ * +  R> 1 +
\          NEXT DROP R@ ( b ?sign) IF NEGATE THEN SWAP
\            ELSE R> R> ( b index) 2DROP ( digit number) 2DROP 0
\            THEN DUP
\        THEN R> ( n ?sign) 2DROP R> BASE ! ;

\ 4.4  Basic I/O
\     : xxx    ...   " A compiled string"  ...   ;                  \ 199
\     : yyy    ...   ." An output string"  ...   ;                  \ 200
\ : ?KEY    ( -- c T  | F ) '?KEY @EXECUTE ;                        \ 201
\ : KEY     ( -- c )   BEGIN ?KEY UNTIL ;                           \ 202
\ : EMIT    ( c -- )   'EMIT @EXECUTE ;                             \ 203
\ : NUF?    ( -- f )   ?KEY DUP IF 2DROP KEY 13 = THEN ;            \ 204
\ : PACE    ( -- )   11  EMIT ;                                     \ 205
\ : SPACE   ( -- )   BL  EMIT ;                                     \ 206
\ : CHARS   ( +n c -- ) \ ???ANS conflict                          \ 207
\      SWAP 0 MAX FOR AFT DUP EMIT THEN NEXT DROP ;                 \ 208
\ : SPACES ( +n -- )   BL CHARS ;                                  \ 209
\
\ : TYPE     ( b u -- ) FOR AFT DUP C@ EMIT 1 + THEN NEXT DROP ;
\
\ : CR      ( -- )     13 EMIT 10 EMIT ;                            \ 210
\ : do$     ( -- a )                                               \ 211
\   R> R@ R> COUNT + ALIGNED >R SWAP >R ;                          \ 212
\ : $"|     ( -- a )    do$ ;                                      \ 213
\ : ."|     ( -- )      do$ COUNT TYPE ; COMPILE-ONLY             \ 214
\ : .R      ( n +n -- ) >R str      R> OVER - SPACES TYPE ;        \ 215
\ : U.R     ( u +n -- ) >R <# #S #> R> OVER - SPACES TYPE ;        \ 216
\ : U.      ( u -- )    <# #S #> SPACE TYPE ;                      \ 217
\ : .       ( n -- )    BASE @ 10 XOR IF U. EXIT THEN str SPACE TYPE ; \ 218
\ : ?       ( a -- )    @ . ;                                      \ 219
\                                                                  \ 220
\
\ 4.5  Parsing
\ : parse  ( b u c -- b u delta ; <string> )                       \ 221
\   tmp !  OVER >R  DUP \ b u u
\   IF 1 -  tmp @ BL =
```

```
\     IF \ b u' \ 'skip'
\        FOR BL OVER C@ - 0< NOT  WHILE 1 +
\        NEXT ( b) R> DROP 0 DUP EXIT \ all delim
\           THEN  R>
\     THEN OVER SWAP \ b' b' u' \ 'scan'
\     FOR tmp @ OVER C@ -  tmp @ BL =
\        IF 0< THEN WHILE 1 +
\     NEXT DUP >R  ELSE R> DROP DUP 1 + >R
\                 THEN OVER -  R>  R> - EXIT
\   THEN       ( b u) OVER R> - ;
\ : PARSE     ( c -- b u ; <string> )                    \ 222
\   >R  TIB >IN @ +  #TIB @ >IN @ -  R> parse >IN +! ;
\ : .(         ( -- ) 41 PARSE TYPE ; IMMEDIATE          \ 223
\ : (          ( -- )  41 PARSE 2DROP ; IMMEDIATE        \ 224
\ : \ ( -- )  #TIB @ >IN ! ; IMMEDIATE                   \ 225
\ : CHAR       ( -- c ) BL PARSE DROP C@ ;               \ 226
\ : TOKEN      ( -- a ; <string> )                       \ 227
\   BL PARSE 31 MIN NP @ OVER - CELL- PACK$ ;            \ 228
\ : WORD       ( c -- a ; <string> ) PARSE HERE PACK$ ;  \ 229

\ 4.6  Dictionary Search
\ : NAME>     ( a -- xt ) CELL- CELL- @ ;                \ 230
\ : SAME?     ( a a u -- a a f \ -0+ )                   \ 231
\   FOR AFT OVER R@ CELLS + @
\           OVER R@ CELLS + @ -  ?DUP
\     IF R> DROP EXIT THEN THEN
\   NEXT 0 ;
\ : find      ( a va -- xt na | a F )                    \ 232
\   SWAP              \ va a
\   DUP C@ 2 / tmp !  \ va a  \ get cell count
\   DUP @ >R          \ va a  \ count byte & 1st char
\   CELL+ SWAP        \ a' va
\   BEGIN @ DUP       \ a' na na
\     IF DUP @ [ =MASK ] LITERAL AND  R@ XOR \ ignore lexicon bits
\       IF CELL+ -1 ELSE CELL+ tmp @ SAME? THEN
\     ELSE R> DROP EXIT
\     THEN
\   WHILE CELL- CELL- \ a' la
\   REPEAT R> DROP SWAP DROP CELL-  DUP NAME> SWAP ;
\ : NAME?     ( a -- xt na | a F )                       \ 233
\   CONTEXT  DUP 2@ XOR IF CELL- THEN >R \ context<>also
\   BEGIN R>  CELL+ DUP >R  @ ?DUP
\   WHILE find   ?DUP
\   UNTIL R> DROP EXIT THEN R> DROP  0 ;

\ 4.7  Terminal
\ : ^H       ( b b b -- b b b )       \ backspace        \ 234
\   >R OVER R> SWAP OVER XOR
\   IF  8 'ECHO @EXECUTE
\       32 'ECHO @EXECUTE        \ distructive
\        8 'ECHO @EXECUTE        \ backspace
\   THEN ;
\ : TAP      ( bot eot cur c -- bot eot cur )            \ 235
```

```
\   DUP 'ECHO @EXECUTE OVER C! 1 + ;
\ : kTAP        ( bot eot cur c -- bot eot cur )            \ 236
\   DUP 13 XOR
\   IF 8 XOR IF BL TAP ELSE ^H THEN EXIT
\   THEN DROP SWAP DROP DUP ;
\ : accept      ( b u -- b u )                              \ 237
\   OVER + OVER
\   BEGIN 2DUP XOR
\   WHILE  KEY  DUP BL -  95 U<
\     IF TAP ELSE 'TAP @EXECUTE THEN
\   REPEAT DROP  OVER - ;
\ : EXPECT      ( b u -- ) 'EXPECT @EXECUTE SPAN ! DROP ;   \ 238
\ : QUERY       ( -- )                                      \ 239
\   TIB 80 'EXPECT @EXECUTE #TIB !  DROP 0 >IN ! ;
```

\ 4.8 Error Handling

```
\ : CATCH       ( ca -- err#/0 )                            \ 240
\                 ( Execute word at ca and set up an error frame for it.)
\   SP@ >R         ( save current stack pointer on return stack )
\   HANDLER @ >R   ( save the handler pointer on return stack )
\   RP@ HANDLER !  ( save the handler frame pointer in HANDLER )
\   ( ca ) EXECUTE ( execute the assigned word
\                     over this safety net )
\  R> HANDLER !    ( normal return from the executed word )
\                  ( restore HANDLER from the return stack )
\  R> DROP         ( discard the saved data stack pointer )
\  0 ;             ( push a no-error flag on data stack )
\ : THROW    ( err# -- err# )                               \ 241
\   ( Reset system to current local error frame an update error flag.)
\   HANDLER @ RP! ( expose latest error handler frame
\                    on return stack )
\   R> HANDLER !   ( restore previously saved error handler frame )
\   R> SWAP >R     ( retrieve the data stack pointer saved )
\   SP!            ( restore the data stack )
\   DROP
\   R> ;           ( retrived err# )
\ : CATCH    ( xt -- 0 | err# )                             \ 242
\   SP@ >R  HANDLER @ >R  RP@ HANDLER !
\   EXECUTE
\   R> HANDLER !  R> DROP  0 ;
\ : THROW ( err# -- err# )                                  \ 243
\   HANDLER @ RP! R> HANDLER !  R> SWAP >R SP! DROP R> ;
\
\   CREATE NULL$ 0 , $," coyote"                            \ 244
\ : ABORT     ( -- ) NULL$ THROW ;                          \ 245
\ : abort"    ( f -- ) IF do$ THROW THEN do$ DROP ;         \ 246
\   BEGIN QUERY [ ' EVAL ] LITERAL   CATCH                  \ 247
\   ?DUP UNTIL                                              \ 248
\ : ABORT   NULL$ THROW ;                                   \ 249
\ : abort"  IF do$ THROW THEN do$ DROP ;                    \ 250
\ : ?STACK  DEPTH 0< IF $" underflow" THROW THEN ;          \ 251
\ : $INTERPRET   ... 'NUMBER @EXECUTE  IF EXIT THEN THROW ; \ 251a
```

```
\ 4.9  Text Interpreter
\ : $INTERPRET   ( a -- )                                        \ 252
\    NAME?  ?DUP
\      IF @ $40 AND
\      ABORT" compile ONLY" EXECUTE EXIT
\        THEN 'NUMBER @EXECUTE IF EXIT THEN THROW ;
\ : [ ( -- ) doLIT $INTERPRET 'EVAL ! ; IMMEDIATE               \ 253
\ : .OK ( -- ) doLIT $INTERPRET 'EVAL @ = IF ." ok" THEN CR ;   \ 254
\ : ?STACK ( -- ) DEPTH 0< ABORT" underflow" ;                  \ 255
\ : EVAL ( -- )                                                 \ 256
\   BEGIN TOKEN DUP C@
\   WHILE 'EVAL @EXECUTE ?STACK
\   REPEAT DROP 'PROMPT @EXECUTE ;


\ 4.10  Shell
\ : PRESET   ( -- ) SP0 @ SP!  TIB #TIB CELL+ ! ;               \ 257
\ : xio      ( a a a -- ) \ reset 'EXPECT 'TAP 'ECHO 'PROMPT    \ 258
\    doLIT accept  'EXPECT 2! 'ECHO 2! ; COMPILE-ONLY
\ : FILE ( -- )                                                 \ 259
\    doLIT PACE  doLIT DROP  doLIT kTAP xio ;
\ : HAND ( -- )                                                 \ 260
\    doLIT .OK   doLIT EMIT  [ kTAP  xio ;
\ CREATE I/O  ' ?RX , ' TX! , \ defaults                        \ 262
\ : CONSOLE ( -- ) I/O 2@ '?KEY 2! HAND ;                       \ 263
\ : QUIT ( -- )                                                 \ 264
\    RP0 @ RP!
\    BEGIN [COMPILE] [
\      BEGIN QUERY doLIT EVAL CATCH ?DUP
\      UNTIL 'PROMPT @ SWAP CONSOLE  NULL$ OVER XOR
\      IF CR #TIB 2@ TYPE
\         CR >IN @ 94 CHARS
\         CR COUNT TYPE ."  ? "
\      THEN doLIT .OK XOR
\      IF $1B EMIT THEN
\    PRESET
\    AGAIN ;

\ 5.0 eForth Compiler
\ 5.1  Interpreter and Compiler
\ : [      ( -- )                                               \ 265
\    [ ' $INTERPRET ] LITERAL
\    'EVAL !       ( vector EVAL to $INTERPRET )
\  ; IMMEDIATE     ( enter into text interpreter mode )
\ : ] ( -- )                                                    \ 266
\    [ ' $COMPILE ] LITERAL
\    'EVAL !     ( vector EVAL to $COMPILE )
\ ;


\ 5.2  Primitive Compiler Words
\ : '        ( -- xt )        TOKEN NAME? IF EXIT THEN THROW ;  \ 267
\ : ALLOT    ( n -- )         CP +! ;                           \ 268
\ : ,        ( w -- )         HERE DUP CELL+ CP ! ! ; \ ???ALIGNED  \ 269
\ : [COMPILE] ( -- ; <string> ) ' , ; IMMEDIATE                \ 270
```

```
\ : COMPILE     ( -- )        R> DUP @ , CELL+ >R ;              \ 271
\ : LITERAL     ( w -- )      COMPILE doLIT , ; IMMEDIATE        \ 272
\ : $,"         ( -- )        34 WORD COUNT ALIGNED CP ! ;       \ 273
\ : RECURSE     ( -- )        LAST @ NAME> , ; IMMEDIATE         \ 274
```

```
\ 5.3  Structures
\ Conditional branch    IF    ... THEN
\                       IF    ... ELSE ...  THEN
\ Finite loop           FOR   ... NEXT
\                       FOR   ... AFT   ... THEN ... NEXT
\ Infinite loop         BEGIN ... AGAIN
\ Indefinite loop       BEGIN ... UNTIL
\                       BEGIN ... WHILE ... REPEAT
\ : <MARK    ( -- a )      HERE ;                                    \ 275
\ : <RESOLVE ( a -- )      , ;                                       \ 276
\ : >MARK    ( -- A )      HERE 0 , ;                                \ 277
\ : >RESOLVE ( A -- )      <MARK SWAP ! ;                            \ 278
\ : FOR      ( -- a )      COMPILE >R <MARK ; IMMEDIATE             \ 279
\ : BEGIN    ( -- a )      <MARK ; IMMEDIATE                        \ 280
\ : NEXT     ( a -- )      COMPILE next <RESOLVE ; IMMEDIATE        \ 281
\ : UNTIL    ( a -- )      COMPILE ?branch <RESOLVE ; IMMEDIATE     \ 282
\ : AGAIN    ( a -- )      COMPILE  branch <RESOLVE ; IMMEDIATE     \ 283
\ : IF       ( -- A )      COMPILE ?branch >MARK ; IMMEDIATE        \ 284
\ : AHEAD    ( -- A )      COMPILE branch >MARK ; IMMEDIATE         \ 285
\ : REPEAT   ( A a -- )    [COMPILE] AGAIN >RESOLVE ; IMMEDIATE     \ 286
\ : THEN     ( A -- )      >RESOLVE ; IMMEDIATE                     \ 287
\ : AFT      ( a -- a A ) DROP [COMPILE] AHEAD [COMPILE] BEGIN SWAP ;
\                          IMMEDIATE                                \ 288
\ : ELSE     ( A -- A )    [COMPILE] AHEAD SWAP [COMPILE] THEN ;    \ 289
\                                IMMEDIATE
\ : WHEN     ( a A -- a A a )  [COMPILE] IF OVER ; IMMEDIATE        \ 290
\ : WHILE    ( a -- A a )      [COMPILE] IF SWAP ; IMMEDIATE        \ 291
\ : ABORT"   ( -- ; <string> ) COMPILE abort" $," ; IMMEDIATE      \ 292
\ : $"       ( -- ; <string> ) COMPILE $"| $," ; IMMEDIATE         \ 293
\ : ."       ( -- ; <string> ) COMPILE ."| $," ; IMMEDIATE         \ 294
```

```
\ 5.4  Compiler
\ : ?UNIQUE  ( a -- a )                                            \ 295
\    DUP NAME? IF ." reDef " OVER COUNT TYPE THEN DROP ;
\ : $,n      ( a -- )                                              \ 296
\    DUP C@
\    IF ?UNIQUE
\    ( na) DUP LAST ! \ for OVERT
\    ( na) HERE ALIGNED SWAP
\    ( cp na) CELL-
\    ( cp la) CURRENT @ @
\    ( cp la na') OVER !
\    ( cp la) CELL- DUP NP ! ( ptr) ! EXIT
\    THEN $" name" THROW ;
\    .( FORTH Compiler )                                           \ 297
\ : $COMPILE ( a -- )                                              \ 298
\    NAME? ?DUP
\    IF @ $80 AND
```

```
\       IF EXECUTE ELSE , THEN EXIT
\       THEN 'NUMBER @EXECUTE
\       IF [COMPILE] LITERAL EXIT
\       THEN THROW ;
\ : OVERT    ( -- ) LAST @ CURRENT @  ! ;                        \ 299
\ : ;        ( -- )                                              \ 300
\       COMPILE EXIT [COMPILE] [ OVERT ; IMMEDIATE
\ : ]        ( -- ) doLIT $COMPILE 'EVAL ! ;                     \ 301
\ : call,    ( xt -- ) \ DTC 8086 relative call                 \ 302
\       $E890 , HERE CELL+ - , ;
\ : :  ( -- ; <string> ) TOKEN $,n doLIT doLIST  call, ] ;      \ 303
\ : IMMEDIATE ( -- ) $80 LAST @ @ OR LAST @ ! ;                 \ 304


\ 5.5  Defining Words
\ : USER ( n -- ; <string> )                                    \ 305
\     TOKEN $,n OVERT
\     doLIT doLIST COMPILE doUSER , ;
\ : CREATE ( -- ; <string> )                                    \ 306
\     TOKEN $,n OVERT
\     doLIT doLIST COMPILE doVAR ;
\ : VARIABLE ( -- ; <string> ) CREATE 0 , ;                     \ 307

\ 6.0  Utilities
\ 6.1  Memory Dump
\ : _TYPE    ( b u -- )                                         \ 307a
\       FOR AFT DUP C@ >CHAR EMIT 1 + THEN NEXT DROP ;
\ : dm+      ( b u -- b )                                       \ 308
\       OVER 4 U.R SPACE FOR AFT DUP C@ 3 U.R 1 + THEN NEXT ;
\ : DUMP     ( b u -- )                                         \ 309
\       BASE @ >R HEX  16 /
\       FOR CR 16 2DUP dm+ ROT ROT 2 SPACES _TYPE NUF? NOT WHILE
\       NEXT ELSE R> DROP THEN DROP  R> BASE ! ;


\ 6.2  Stack Tools
\ : .S      ( -- )    CR DEPTH FOR AFT R@ PICK . THEN NEXT ." <sp" ;  \ 310
\ : .BASE   ( -- )    BASE @ DECIMAL DUP . BASE ! ;                   \ 311
\ : .FREE   ( -- )    CP 2@ - U. ;                                    \ 312
\ : !CSP    ( -- )    SP@ CSP ! ;                                     \ 313
\ : ?CSP    ( -- )    SP@ CSP @ XOR ABORT" stack depth" ;             \ 314


\ 6.3  Dictionary Dump
\ : >NAME   ( xt -- na | F )                                    \ 315
\   CURRENT
\   BEGIN CELL+ @ ?DUP WHILE 2DUP
\     BEGIN @ DUP WHILE 2DUP NAME> XOR
\     WHILE CELL-
\     REPEAT      THEN SWAP DROP ?DUP
\   UNTIL SWAP DROP SWAP DROP EXIT THEN DROP 0 ;
\ : .ID     ( a -- )                                            \ 316
\     ?DUP IF COUNT $01F AND _TYPE EXIT THEN ." {noName}" ;
\ : SEE ( -- ; <string> )                                       \ 317
\     ' CR CELL+
\     BEGIN CELL+ DUP @ DUP IF >NAME THEN ?DUP
```

```
\       IF SPACE .ID ELSE DUP @ U. THEN NUF?
\     UNTIL DROP ;
\ : WORDS    ( -- )                                          \ 318
\   CR  CONTEXT @
\   BEGIN @ ?DUP
\   WHILE DUP SPACE .ID CELL- NUF?
\   UNTIL DROP THEN ;
```

```
\ 6.4  Startup
\ : VER ( -- u ) $101 ;                                      \ 319
\ : hi ( -- )                                                \ 320
\     !IO BASE @ HEX \ initialize IO device & sign on
\     CR ." eFORTH V" VER <# # # 46 HOLD # #> TYPE
\     CR ;
\ : EMPTY ( -- )                                             \ 321
\     FORTH CONTEXT @ DUP CURRENT 2!  6 CP 3 MOVE OVERT ;
\ CREATE 'BOOT   ' hi , \ application vector                 \ 322
\ : COLD ( -- )                                              \ 323
\     BEGIN
\        U0 UP 74 CMOVE
\        PRESET  'BOOT @EXECUTE
\        FORTH CONTEXT @ DUP CURRENT 2! OVERT
\        QUIT
\     AGAIN ;
```

```
\ 6.5  ColdBoot from DOS
\ ;; Main entry points and COLD start data                  \ 324
\ MAIN     SEGMENT
\ ASSUME  CS:MAIN,DS:MAIN,ES:MAIN,SS:MAIN
\ ORG   COLDD              ;beginning of cold boot
\ ORIG:   MOV   AX,CS
\         MOV   DS,AX          ;DS is same as CS
\         CLI                   ;disable interrupts, old 808x CPU bug
\         MOV   SS,AX          ;SS is same as CS
\         MOV   SP,SPP         ;initialize SP
\         STI                   ;enable interrupts
\         MOV   BP,RPP         ;initialize RP
\         MOV   AL,023H         ;interrupt 23H
\         MOV   DX,OFFSET CTRLC
\         MOV   AH,025H        ;MS-DOS set interrupt vector
\         INT   021H
\         CLD                 ;direction flag, increment
\         JMP   COLD          ;to high level cold start
\ CTRLC:IRET                  ;control C interrupt routine
\ ; COLD start moves the following to USER variables.       \ 325
\ ; MUST BE IN SAME ORDER AS USER VARIABLES.
\ $ALIGN           ;align to cell boundary

\ UZERO:  DW   4 DUP (0)   ; reserved
\         DW   SPP           ;SP0
\         DW   RPP           ;RP0
\         DW   QRX         ;'?KEY
\         DW   TXSTO       ;'EMIT
```

```
\          DW    ACCEP      ;'EXPECT
\          DW    KTAP       ;'TAP
\          DW    TXSTO      ;'ECHO
\          DW    DOTOK      ;'PROMPT
\          DW    BASEE        ;BASE
\          DW    0            ;tmp
\          DW    0            ;SPAN
\          DW    0            ;>IN
\          DW    0          ;#TIB
\          DW    TIBB       ;TIB
\          DW    0          ;CSP
\          DW    INTER        ;'EVAL
\          DW    NUMBQ        ;'NUMBER
\          DW    0            ;HLD
\          DW    0            ;HANDLER
\          DW    0              ;CONTEXT pointer
\          DW    VOCSS DUP (0)    ;vocabulary stack
\          DW    0              ;CURRENT pointer
\          DW    0              ;vocabulary link pointer
\          DW    CTOP       ;CP
\          DW    NTOP       ;NP
\          DW    LASTN      ;LAST
\ ULAST:
```

\ 7.0   Some Final Thoughts
\ Congratulations, if you reach this point the first time.
\ As you can see, we have traversed a complete Forth system
\   from the beginning to the end,
\   and it is not as difficult as you might have thought before you began.
\ But, think again what we have accomplished.
\   It is a complete operating system with an integrated interpreter
\   and an integrated compiler all together.
\ If you look in the memory, the whole system is less than 7 Kbytes.
\   What else can you do with 7 Kbytes these days?
\ Forth is like Zen. It is simple, it is accessible,
\   and it can be understood in its entirety
\   without devoting your whole life to it.
\ Is this the end? Not really. There are many topics important in Forth,
\   but we had chosen to ignore in this simple model.
\ They include multitasking, virtual memory, interrupt control,
\   programming style, source code management, and yes, metacompilation.
\ However, these topics can be considered advanced applications of Forth.
\ Once the fundamental principles in Forth are understood,
\   these topics can be subject for further investigations at your leisure.
\ Forth is not an end to itself.
\ It is only a tool, as useful as the user intends it to be.
\ The most important thing is how the user can use it to solve his problems
\   and build useful applications.
\ What eForth gives you is the understanding of this tool.
\   It is up to you to make use of it.

\ #### V3 2014_06_28   v5_2018_10_19 eForthOverview5_A5v4_CODE_ONLY v7_shorted

The Forth Bookshelf contains more of Ting's documentations as eBook / print book.
Just follow the link
https://www.amazon.co.uk/Juergen-Pintaske/e/B00N8HVEZM

Dr. Chen-Hanson Ting

Introduction:

Retired chemist-turned-engineer

How long have you been interested in Forth: 32 years

Biography:

PhD in chemistry, University of Chicago, 1965.

Professor of chemistry in Taiwan until 1975.

Firmware engineer in Silicon Valley until retirement in 2000.
Still actively composing Forth Haikus.

Custodian of the eForth systems since 1990,
still maintaining eForth systems for Arduino, MSP430,
and various ARM microcontrollers.

Author of eP8, eP16, eP24, and eP32 microcontrollers in VHDL, which were
implemented on several FPGA chips.

Offete Enterprises, started in 1975, and is now formally closed.

However, Dr. Ting can still be contacted via email chenhting@yahoo.com.tw

Formatted and published by ExMark – Juergen Pintaske – Sept. 2016 / October 2018

Made in the USA
San Bernardino, CA
10 April 2019